The Art of Being

Erich Fromm

The Art of Being

Foreword by Rainer Funk

Constable · London

First published in Great Britain 1993
by Constable, an imprint of Constable & Robinson Limited
3 Lanchesters, 162 Fulham Palace Road
London W6 9ER
Copyright © 1993 by Erich Fromm
The right of Erich Fromm to be
identified as the author of this work
has been asserted by him in accordance with
the Copyright, Designs and Patents Act 1988
ISBN 9780094720909
Reprinted 1994, 1995, 1997, 1998, 2001, 2006, 2007
Printed and bound in Great Britain by
Mackays of Chatham plc, Chatham Kent

A CIP catalogue record of this book
is available from the British Library

Contents

PART V

PART VI

Editor's Foreword

Between 1974 and 1976, while working on the book *To Have Or to Be?* at his home in Locarno, Switzerland, the aged Erich Fromm wrote far more manuscript and chapters than were actually used in the book, which was published in 1976. Some of these chapters are contained in the present volume. They deal entirely with the "steps toward being" that the individual can take in order to learn "the art of being."

Fromm withdrew the chapters on "Steps toward Being" from the typescript shortly before the typesetting of *To Have Or to Be?* because he believed that his book could be misunderstood to mean that each individual has *only* to search for spiritual well-being in the awareness, development, and analysis of himself without changing the economic realities that produce the having mode. The roots of the mass phenomenon of orientation toward "having," which are typical of a luxuriant society that has everything, were to be sought for in the economic, political, and social realities of modern industrial society, especially in its organization of labor, and in its modes of production.

Despite the fact that our orientation toward having is rooted in the structural realities of today's industrial culture, the overcoming of these realities consists in rediscovering man's own psychic, intellectual, and physical powers and in his possibilities of self-determination. For this reason, these "Steps toward Being" are now being published. They are intended to be a guide to productive self-awareness.

Recent trends have certainly made it clear that the awareness, realization, development, etc., of one's self almost always mean something other than the enhancement of one's own subjective powers. Today, by and large, individual narcissism is simply being strengthened and the inability to reason and to love (which, according to Fromm, are characteristics of an orientation toward being) entrenched, as techniques of self-awareness offer new crutches of orientation toward having.

The following summary of some of the statements made earlier in *To Have Or to Be?* is meant not to be a substitute for having read that book, but rather to remind all who have read it of its most important thoughts.

Erich Fromm understood the alternatives having or being to be "two fundamental modes of existence, or two different kinds of orientation toward self and the world, two different types of character structure whose respective dominance determines the totality of how a person thinks, feels, and acts." (*To Have Or to Be?*, p. 24.)—If one investigates all the possible ways in which a person can orient his life, then one comes to this conclusion: In the end, a person orients his life either toward having or toward being.

What does it mean when someone ultimately orients his or her life toward having?

Whoever orients his or her life toward having determines oneself, one's existence, one's meaning of life, and one's way of life according to what one has, what that person can have, and what one can have more of. Now, there is almost nothing that could not become an object of having and of the desire to have: material things of all types—one's own house, money, stocks, artworks, books, stamps, coins, and other things that, in part, can be amassed with "the passion of a collector."

People, too, can become the object of having or of the desire to have. Of course, one does not say that one takes possession of another person and considers that person one's property. One is more "considerate" in this regard and prefers to say that one is concerned about others and takes responsibility for them. But it is well known that whoever has the responsibility for others also has the right to dispose of them. Thus, children, the disabled, the old, the sick, and those in need of care are taken possession of and considered to be a part of one's own self—and woe! should the sick become healthy and the child wish to decide for itself. Being determined by the having mode then becomes obvious.

As though it were not enough that other people can be "had," we also determine the conduct of our lives by taking on or acquiring virtues and honors. All that matters to us is that we have esteem, a certain image, health, beauty, or youth, and when this is no longer possible, then we at least want to have "experience" or "memories." Convictions of a political, ideological, and religious nature can also be acquired as possessions and staunchly defended—to the point of bloodshed. Everything is made dependent upon whether one is in possession of the truth or whether one is in the right.

Virtually anything can be possessed if a person orients his way of life toward having. The issue is not whether one does or does not have something, but rather whether a person's heart is set on what he or she does or does not have. Orientation toward not-having is a having orientation, too. Fromm is not advocating asceticism; orientation toward "being" is precisely what is *not* identical with orientation toward "not-having." The perpetual question concerns the position that having or not-having holds in the determination of one's purpose in life and in the determination of one's own identity. It is often difficult to distinguish whether someone possesses something in the having mode of existence or, to quote Fromm, whether someone "possesses as if he were not possessing." Yet each person can quickly test himself or herself by asking what he or she finds particularly valuable, thereby getting an idea of what would happen if he or she were to lose what was important and valuable: whether he or she would lose the ground from under his or her feet and whether life would then become meaningless. If one can then no longer feel any self-reliance or self-value (intrinsic to oneself), if life and work are no longer worth anything, then one is determining life according to an orientation toward having: having a fine vocation, obedient children, a good rapport, profound insights, better arguments, and so forth.

The person who is oriented toward having always makes use of crutches rather than his or her own two feet. That person uses an external object in order to exist, in order to be oneself as he or she wishes. He or she is himself or herself only insofar as that person *has* something. The individual determines being as a subject according to the having of an object. He or she is possessed by objects, and thus by the object of having them.

At the same time, the metaphor of crutches replacing one's own feet makes apparent what is meant by a different orientation, that of being. Just as a person has a physical capacity for self-reliance, which can be replaced with crutches if need be, so does one have psychic abilities for self-reliance, too: a capacity for love, a capacity for reason, and a capacity for productive activity. But it is also possible for a person to replace those innate psychic powers with an orientation toward having, such that a capacity for love, reason, and productive activity depends upon the possession of those objects of having upon which the heart is set.

Love, reason, and productive activity are one's own psychic forces that arise and grow only to the extent that they are practiced; they cannot be consumed, bought, or possessed like objects of having, but can only be practiced, exercised, ventured upon, performed. In contradistinction to objects of having—which are expended when they are used up—love, reason, and productive activity grow and increase when they are shared and used.

Orientation toward being always means that one's purpose in life is oriented toward one's own psychic forces. One recognizes, becomes acquainted with, and assimilates the fact that the unknown and the strange in oneself, and in the external world, are characteristic of *one's own self.* By learning this, one attains a greater and more comprehensive relationship with one's self and one's environment.

In *To Have Or to Be?* Fromm proceeded from the observation that today's orientation toward having is a mass phenomenon founded in the economic and social actualities of a society that has too much and that can, therefore, succumb to the temptation of letting itself be determined or defined by having. The enormous loss of individuals' own psychic forces can be found in the structural realities of present-day economics, of present-day organization of labor, and of present-day social life.

If the roots of the fateful development of the individual are to be sought for primarily in the socio-economically determined lot of today's person, then it is valid to proceed on the basis of these roots and to understand the individual as having always been socialized. That is why Fromm replaced the chapter on the "Steps Toward Being" with his suggestions for structural change. And

that is why an individual's efforts to shift from an orientation
toward having to an orientation toward being can make sense
only if those efforts simultaneously change the structure of one's
own setting. In vocational activity, in the organization of one's
own work, and in political and societal self-awareness, the guid-
ing values of one's own socio-economic way of life must be
changed so that one can genuinely experience one's own psychic
forces of reason, love, and productive activity and so that those
powers can grow by use.

Our attempt to attain self-awareness and self-development, to
attain a view of ourselves and of our world that truly corresponds
to inner and external reality, is connected with the liberation of
our socio-economic way of life. Indeed, "Only to the degree
that the *practice* of life is freed from its contradictions and its
irrationality can the map correspond to reality," the author said
in *To Have Or to Be?*

In the present volume, Erich Fromm first shows the false paths
of self-awareness, just as he clearly recognized and identified them
as such years ago, with all the pathos of a didact. Yet he then suggests ways of gaining self-awareness and shares with us the steps
toward being that he himself has practiced daily, giving very exten-
sive attention to *self-analysis* as an application of *psychoanalysis*.

Because the present work, available here for the first time, was
not prepared for publication by Fromm himself, there was a
need for occasional supplementation both of the division and
systematization of the text as well as of the chapter headings.

Rainer Funk
Tübingen (Germany), 1992

(Translated by Lance W. Garmer)

PART I

1. On the Art of Being

In the first part of this book I have tried to describe the nature of the *having* and of the *being* modes of existence, and the consequences that the dominance of either mode has for man's well-being. We had concluded that the full humanization of man requires the breakthrough from the possession-centered to the activity-centered orientation, from selfishness and egotism to solidarity and altruism. In the second part of the book I want to make some practical suggestions concerning the steps that might be helpful as preparations for the effort to move toward this humanization.

The discussion of steps in the practice of the art of living must begin with the question on the answer to which all practice depends: What is the goal of living? What is life's meaning for man?

But is this really a meaningful question? Is there a reason for wanting to live, and would we rather not live if we had no such reason? The fact is that all living beings, animals and men, want to live, and this wish is paralyzed only under exceptional circumstances, such as unbearable pain or (in man) by the presence of passions such as love, hate, pride, loyalty that can be stronger than the wish to live. It seems that nature—or if you will, the process of evolution—has endowed every living being with the wish to live, and whatever he believes to be his reasons are only secondary thoughts by which he rationalizes this biologically given impulse.

We do of course need to acknowledge theoretical ideas of evo-

1

lution. Meister Eckhart has made the same point in a simpler, poetic way:

"If you ask a good man, "Why do you love God?" you will be answered: "I don't know—because he *is* God!""

"Why do you love truth?"

"For truth's sake."

"Why do you love justice?"

"For the sake of justice!"

"Why do you love goodness?"

"For goodness' sake!"

"And why do you live?"

"On my honor, I don't know—I like to live!"[1]

That we want to live, that we like to live, are facts that require no explanation. But if we ask *how* we want to live—what we seek from life, what makes life meaningful for us—then indeed we deal with questions (and they are more or less identical) to which people will give many different answers. Some will say they want love, others will choose power, others security, others sensuous pleasure and comfort, others fame; but most would probably agree in the statement that what they want is *happiness*. This is also what most philosophers and theologians have declared to be the aim of human striving. However, if happiness covers such different, and mostly mutually exclusive, contents as the ones just mentioned, it becomes an abstraction and thus rather useless. What matters is to examine what the term "happiness" means— for the layman as well as for the philosopher.

Even among the different concepts of happiness there is still a view shared by most thinkers: We are happy if our wishes are fulfilled, or, to put it differently, if we have what we want. The differences between the various views consist in the answer to the question "What are those needs the fulfillment of which brings about happiness?" We come thus to the point at which *the question of the aim and meaning of life leads us to the problem of the nature of human needs.*

---

1. *Meister Eckhart: A Modern Translation,* tr. R. B. Blakney (New York: Harper Torchbooks, Harper & Row, 1941), p. 242.

By and large, there are two opposing positions. The first, and today almost exclusively held, position is that a need is defined entirely *subjectively;* it is the striving for something I want badly enough so that we have a right to call it a need, the satisfaction of which gives pleasure. In this definition the question is not raised what the source of the need is. It is not asked whether, as with hunger and thirst, it has a physiological root, or, like the need for refined food and drink, for art, for theoretical thought, it is a need rooted in the social and cultural development of man, or whether it is a socially induced need like that for cigarettes, automobiles, or innumerable gadgets, or, finally, whether it is a pathological need like that for such behaviors as sadism or masochism.

Nor, in this first view, is the question raised what effect the satisfaction of the need has on a person—whether it enriches his life and contributes to his growth or whether it weakens him, stifles him, prevents growth, and is self-destructive. Whether a person enjoys the satisfaction of his desire to listen to Bach, or that of his sadism by controlling or hurting helpless people, is supposed to be a matter of taste; as long as this is what a person has a need for, happiness consists in the satisfaction of this need. The only exceptions that usually are made are those cases in which the satisfaction of a need severely damages other people or the social usefulness of the person himself. Thus the need to destroy or the need to take drugs are usually not supposed to be needs that can claim their legitimacy from the fact that their satisfaction might produce pleasure.

The opposite (or second) position is fundamentally different. It focuses on the question of whether a need is conducive to man's growth and well-being or whether it hobbles and damages him. It speaks of such needs as are rooted in man's nature and are conducive to his growth and self-fulfillment. In this second concept the purely subjective nature of happiness is replaced by an objective, normative one. Only the fulfillment of desires that are in man's interests leads to happiness.

In the first instance I say: "I am happy if I get all the pleasure I want"; in the second: "I am happy if I get what I ought to want, provided I want to attain an optimum of self-completion."

It need not be emphasized that this last version is unacceptable from the standpoint of conventional scientific thinking because it introduces a norm—i.e., a value judgment—into the picture and hence seems to deprive the affirmation of its objective validity. The question arises, however, whether it is true that a norm has objective validity. Can we not speak of a "nature of man," and if this is so, does not an objectively definable nature of man lead to the assumption that its aim is the same as that of all living beings, namely, its most perfect functioning and the fullest realization of its potentialities? Does it then not follow that certain norms are conducive to this aim while others hamper it?

This is indeed well understood by any gardener. The aim of the life of a rosebush is to be all that is inherent as potentiality in the rosebush: that its leaves are well developed and that its flower is the most perfect rose that can grow out of this seed. The gardener knows, then, in order to reach this aim he must follow certain norms that have been empirically found. The rosebush needs a specific kind of soil, of moisture, of temperature, of sun and shade. It is up to the gardener to provide these things if he wants to have beautiful roses. But even without his help the rosebush tries to provide itself with the optimum of needs. It can do nothing about moisture and soil, but it can do something about sun and temperature by growing "crooked," in the direction of the sun, provided there is such an opportunity. Why would not the same hold true for the human species?

Even if we had no theoretical knowledge about the reasons for the norms that are conducive to man's optimal growth and functioning, experience tells us just as much as it tells the gardener. Therein lies the reason that all great teachers of man have arrived at essentially the same norms for living, the essence of these norms being that the overcoming of greed, illusions, and hate, and the attainment of love and compassion, are the conditions for attaining optimal being. Drawing conclusions from empirical evidence, even if we cannot explain the evidence theoretically, is a perfectly sound and by no means "unscientific" method, although the scientists' ideal will remain, to discover the laws behind the empirical evidence.

Now, those who insist that all so-called value judgments in reference to human happiness have no theoretical foundation do not raise the same objection with regard to a physiological problem, although logically the case is not different. Assuming a person has a craving for sweets and cakes, becomes fat and endangers his health, they do not say: "If eating constitutes his greatest happiness, he should go on with it and not persuade himself, or let himself be persuaded by others, to renounce this pleasure." They recognize this craving as something different from normal desires, precisely because it damages the organism. This qualification is not called subjective—or a value judgment or unscientific—simply because everyone knows the connection between overeating and health. But, then, everyone also knows today a great deal about the pathological and damaging character of irrational passions such as the craving for fame, power, possessions, revenge, control, and can indeed qualify these needs as damaging, on an equally theoretical and clinical basis.

One has only to think of the "manager sickness," peptic ulcers, which is the result of wrong living, the stress produced by overambitiousness, dependence on success, lack of a truly personal center. There is much data that goes beyond the connection between such wrong attitudes and somatic sickness. In recent decades a number of neurologists, such as C. von Monakow, R. B. Livingston, and Heinz von Foerster, have suggested that man is equipped with a neurologically built-in "biological" conscience in which norms such as cooperation and solidarity, a search for truth and for freedom are rooted. These conceptions are based on considerations of the theory of evolution.[2] I myself have attempted to demonstrate that the principal human norms are conditions for the full growth of the human being, while many of the purely subjective desires are objectively harmful.[3]

The goal of living as it is understood in the following pages

---

2. Cf. the discussion of these views in E. Fromm, *The Anatomy of Human Destructiveness* (New York: Holt Rinehart and Winston, 1973).

3. Cf. the same volume and E. Fromm, *Man for Himself* (New York: Rinehart & Co., 1947).

can be postulated on different levels. Most generally speaking, it can be defined as developing oneself in such a way as to come closest to the *model* of human nature (Spinoza) or, in other words, to grow optimally according to the conditions of human existence and thus to *become* fully what one potentially *is;* to let reason or experience guide us to the understanding of what norms are conducive to well-being, given the nature of man that reason enables us to understand (Thomas Aquinas).

Perhaps the most fundamental form of expressing the goal and the meaning of living is common to the tradition of both the Far East and Near East (and Europe): the "Great Liberation"— liberation from the dominance of greed (in all its forms) and from the shackles of illusions. This double aspect of liberation is to be found in systems such as Indian Vedic religion, Buddhism, and Chinese and Japanese Zen Buddhism, as well as in a more mythical form of God as supreme king in Judaism and Christianity. It finds its crowning development (in the Near East and West) in Christian and Muslim mystics, in Spinoza, and in Marx. In all these teachings, inner liberation—freedom from the shackles of greed and illusions—is inseparably tied to the optimal development of reason; that is to say, reason understood as the use of thought with the aim to know the world *as it is* and in contrast to "manipulating intelligence," which is the use of thought for the purpose of satisfying one's need. This relation of freedom from greed and the primacy of reason is intrinsically necessary. Our reason functions only to the degree to which it is not flooded by greed. The person who is the prisoner of his irrational passions loses the capacity for objectivity and is necessarily at the mercy of his passions; he rationalizes when he believes he is expressing the truth.

The concept of liberation (in its two dimensions) as the goal of life has been lost in industrial society, or rather it has been narrowed down and thus distorted. Liberation has been exclusively applied to liberation from *outside forces;* by the middle class from feudalism, by the working class from capitalism, by the peoples in Africa and Asia from imperialism. The only kind of liberation that was emphasized was that from outer forces; it was essentially *political liberation*.[4]

Indeed, liberation from outer domination is necessary, because such domination cripples the inner man, with the exception of rare individuals. But the one-sidedness of the emphasis on outer liberation also did great damage. In the first place, the liberators often transformed themselves into new rulers, only mouthing the ideologies of freedom. Second, political liberation could hide the fact that new un-freedom developed, but in hidden and anonymous forms. This is the case in Western democracy, where political liberation hides the fact of dependency in many disguises. (In the Soviet countries the domination has been more overt.) Most importantly, one forgot entirely that man can be a slave even without being put in chains—the reverse of an oft-repeated religious statement that man can be free even when he is in chains. This may sometimes, in exceedingly rare cases, be true—however, it is not a statement that is significant for our times; but that man can be a slave without chains is of crucial importance in our situation today. The outer chains have simply been put inside of man. The desires and thoughts that the suggestion-apparatus of society fills him with, chain him more thoroughly than outer chains. This is so because man can at least be aware of outer chains but be unaware of inner chains, carrying them with the illusion that he is free. He can try to overthrow the outer chains, but how can he rid himself of chains of whose existence he is unaware?

Any attempt to overcome the possibly fatal crisis of the industrialized part of the world, and perhaps of the human race, must begin with the understanding of the nature of both outer and inner chains; it must be based on the liberation of man in the classic, humanist sense as well as in the modern, political and

---

4. I am speaking here of the popular concepts and feelings. If we consider the enlightenment philosophy with its motto *sapere aude* ("dare to know") and of the philosophers' concern with *inner* freedom, the concept of freedom was of course not mainly a political one.

social sense. The Church still by and large speaks only of inner liberation, and political parties, from liberals to communists, speak only about outer liberation. History has clearly shown that one ideology without the other leaves man dependent and crippled. The only realistic aim is *total* liberation, a goal that may well be called *radical* (or *revolutionary*) *humanism*.

Just as liberation has been distorted in industrial society, so too has the concept of reason. Since the beginning of the Renaissance, the main object that reason has tried to grasp was Nature, and the marvels of technique were the fruits of the new science. But man himself ceased to be the object of study, except, more recently, in the alienated forms of psychology, anthropology, and sociology. More and more he was degraded to a mere tool for economic goals. In the less than three centuries following Spinoza, it was Freud who was the first to again make the "inner man" the object of science, even though Freud was handicapped by the narrow framework of bourgeois materialism.

The crucial question today is, as I see it, whether we can reconstitute the classic concept of inner and outer liberation with the concept of reason in its two aspects, as applied to nature (science) and applied to man (self-awareness).

*   *   *

Before beginning to make suggestions concerning certain preparatory steps in the learning of the art of living, I want to make sure that there may be no misunderstanding of my intentions. If the reader has expected that this chapter was a short prescription for learning the art of living, he had better stop here. All I want—and am able—to offer are suggestions in what direction the reader will find answers, and to sketch tentatively what some of them are. The only thing that might compensate the reader for the incompleteness of what I have to say is that I shall speak only of methods I have practiced and experienced myself.

This principle of presentation implies that I shall not try in the following chapters to write about all or even only about the most important methods of preparatory practices. Other methods such as Yoga or Zen practice, meditation centered around a repeated word, the Alexander, the Jacobson, and the Feldenkrais methods of relaxation are left out. To write systematically about all methods would require at least a volume by itself, and aside from this I would not be capable of writing such a compendium because I believe one cannot write about experiences that one has not experienced.

Indeed, this chapter could be ended right here by saying: Read the writings of Masters of Living, learn to understand the true meaning of their words, form your own conviction of what you want to do with your life; and get over the naïve idea that you need no master, no guide, no model, that you can find out in a lifetime what the greatest minds of the human species have discovered in many thousands of years—and each one of them building with the stones and sketches their predecessors left them. As one of the greatest masters of living—Meister Eckhart—said: "How can anyone live without being instructed in the art of living and of dying?"

Yet I am not ending the book here, but shall try to present in a simple form some ideas I have learned studying the great masters.

Before even considering some of the steps that are helpful, one should be made aware of the main obstacles that stand in the way. If one is unaware of what to avoid, all of one's efforts will be in vain.

PART II

2. Great Shams

Perhaps the most difficult obstacle to learning the art of living is what I would call the "great sham." Not as if it were restricted to the field of human enlightenment; on the contrary, the latter is only one of the manifestations of the great sham pervading all spheres of our society. Phenomena such as products with built-in obsoleteness, products that are overpriced or actually useless if not harmful to the buyer, advertising that is a blend of a little truth and much falsehood, and many other social phenomena are part of the great fake—of which the law prosecutes only the most drastic forms. Speaking merely of commodities, their real value is covered up by the value that advertising and the name and greatness of their producers suggest. How could it be otherwise in a system whose basic principle is that production is directed by the interest in maximal profit and not by the interest in maximal usefulness for human beings?

The great sham in the sphere of politics has become more visible recently through Watergate and the conduct of the Vietnam War, with its untrue statement about "near victory" or direct faking (as in false reports of aerial attacks). Yet only the tip of the iceberg of political sham has been exposed.

In the spheres of art and literature the sham is also rampant. The public, even the educated public, has largely lost its capacity to know the difference between what is genuine and what is fake. This defect is caused by several factors. Foremost of all is the purely cerebral orientation of most people. They read or listen to only *words* and intellectual concepts, and do not listen "with a third ear" for proof of the author's authenticity. To give an

11

example: In the literature on Zen Buddhism there are writers such as D. T. Suzuki, whose authenticity is beyond doubt; he speaks of what he has experienced. The very fact of this authenticity makes his books often difficult to read, because it is of the essence of Zen not to give answers that are rationally satisfying. There are some other books, which seem to portray the *thoughts* of Zen properly but whose authors are mere intellectuals whose experience is shallow. Their books are easier to understand, but they do not convey the essential quality of Zen. Yet I have found that most people who claim to have a serious interest in Zen have not noticed the decisive difference in quality between Suzuki and others.

The other reason for our difficulty to discern the difference between the authentic and the sham lies in the hypnotic attraction of power and fame. If the name of a man or the title of a book is made famous by clever publicity, the average person is willing to believe the work's claims. This process is greatly helped by another factor: In a completely commercialized society in which salability and optimal profit constitute the core values, and in which every person experiences himself as "capital" that he has to invest on the market with the aim of optimal profit (success), his inner value counts as little as that of a dental cream or a patent medicine. Whether he is kind, intelligent, productive, courageous matters little if these qualities have not been of use to make him successful. On the other hand, if he is only mediocre as a person, writer, artist, or whatever, and is a narcissistic, aggressive, drunken, obscene headline maker, he will—given some talent—easily become one of the "leading artists or writers" of the day. Of course, not only he is involved: The art dealers, literary agents, P.R. men, publishers all are interested financially in his success. He is "made" by them, and once he is a nationally advertised writer, painter, singer, once he is a "celebrity," he is a great man—just as the soap powder is the best whose name you cannot help remembering if you are a TV viewer. Of course, fake and fraud are nothing new; they have always existed. But there was perhaps no time in which the fact of being in the public eye was of such exclusive importance.

With these examples, we touch upon the sector of the great sham that is most important in the context of this book: the sham *in the field of man's salvation,* of his well-being, inner growth, and happiness.

I must confess here that I was very hesitant to write this chapter and was even tempted to leave it out after I had written it. The reason for this hesitancy lies in the fact that there are almost no words left in this field that have not been commercialized, corrupted, and otherwise misused. Words such as "human growth" or "growth potential," "self-actualization," "experiencing versus thinking," "the here and now," and many others have been cheapened by various writers and groups, and even used in advertising copy. Must I not fear that the reader will connect certain ideas I am writing about with others that have the opposite meaning, just because some words are the same? Is it not more adequate to stop writing in this field altogether, or to use mathematical symbols that are defined in a separate list? I beg the reader to be aware of the fact that words, in and by themselves, have no reality, except in terms of the context in which they are used, in terms of the intentions and the character of the one who uses them. If they are read in a one-dimensional way, without a depth perspective, they hide ideas rather than communicate them.

Before beginning even a brief sketch, I want to state that in speaking of sham I do not imply that the leaders and practitioners in various movements are consciously dishonest or intend to deceive the public. Although there are some for whom this holds true, I believe that many intend to do good and believe in the usefulness of their spiritual commodities. Yet there is not merely conscious and intended sham; the socially more dangerous is the swindle in which the performers honestly *believe,* whether it is to plan a war or to offer the way to happiness. Indeed, certain things have to be said, even at the risk of my being taken as personally attacking well-meaning people.

There is, in fact, little reason for personal attacks, since these merchants of salvation only satisfy a widespread demand. How could it be different? People are confused and unsure, they seek

answers to guide them to joy, tranquillity, self-knowledge, salvation—but they also demand that it be easy to learn, that it require
little or no effort, that results be quickly obtained.

In the twenties and thirties a new movement emerged built
upon the genuine interest of a small number of people in new
and hitherto unpopular ideas. These ideas were organized
around two central issues: the liberation of the body and the
liberation of the mind from the shackles into which conventional
life had bound and distorted them.

The first trend had two sources; one was psychoanalytic.
Georg Groddek was the first to use massage to loosen up the
body and thus help a patient to get rid of tensions and repres-
sions. Wilhelm Reich went the same way more systematically
and with greater theoretical awareness of what he was doing: the
breaking of the resistance that defends the repressed by breaking
down the cramped and distorted bodily posture that functions
as a protective defense against de-repression. Reich's work was
based on various methods of body awareness starting with the
work of Elsa Gindler in the 1920s.

The second trend, the liberation of the mind, was centered
mostly on Eastern ideas, particularly certain forms of Yoga, Zen
Buddhism, and Buddhist meditation. All the ideas and methods,
in which only a few people were interested, are genuine and
important and have been of great help to a number of persons
who did not expect to find an easy shortcut to salvation.

In the fifties and sixties a much larger number of people were
looking for new ways to happiness, and a mass market began
to form. Especially California was a fruitful soil for mixing up
legitimate methods, like some of those mentioned, with cheap
methods in which sensitivity, joy, insight, self-knowledge,
greater affectiveness, and relaxation were promised in short
courses, in a kind of spiritual smorgasbord program. Today there
is nothing missing in this program; you can have sensitivity training, group therapy, Zen, T'ai Chi Chuan, almost anything under
the sun, in pleasant surroundings and together with others who
suffer from the same troubles: lack of genuine contact and genu-

ine feeling. From college students to business executives, everybody finds what he wants, with little effort required.

With some dishes of the smorgasbord, such as "sensory awareness," there is nothing the matter with the teaching, my only criticism being the atmosphere in which it is taught. In other endeavors the sham lies in the superficiality of the teaching, especially when it pretends to be based on the insight of the great masters. But perhaps the greatest sham is that what is promised—explicitly or implicitly—is a deep change in personality, while what is given is momentary improvement of symptoms or, at best, stimulation of energy and some relaxation. In essence, these methods are means of feeling better and of becoming better adjusted to society without a basic change in character.

This Californian movement, however, is insignificant by comparison with the mass production of spiritual goods organized by and around Indian "Gurus." The most stunning success has been that of the movement called Transcendental Meditation (T.M.), whose leader is the Indian Maharishi Mahesh Yogi. This guru seized upon a very old Indian traditional idea, that of meditation over a mantra—a mantra usually being a word from Hindu scripture that is supposed to have special significance (like "OM" in the Upanishads) if one concentrates on it. This concentration results in relaxation, and in lessening of tension, and in a feeling of well-being that accompanies the relaxation. T.M. can be practiced without mystifications by using English words such as "Be still," "Love," "One," "Peace," or any others that recommend themselves. If practiced regularly every day in a relaxed position, with closed eyes, for about twenty minutes, it has apparently a marked effect of quietness, relaxation, and increase in energy. (Since I have not practiced it myself so far, I only rely on credible reports by those who have.)[1]

Maharishi did not invent this method, but he has invented

---

1. Dr. Herbert Benson, chief of the hypertension section at Boston's Beth-Israel Hospital, reports on remarkable decrease of blood pressure in hypertensive patients (*Newsweek,* May 5, 1975).

how it can be packaged and marketed. In the first place, he sells the mantras, alleging that for each individual that mantra is chosen which fits the individuality of the customer. (Even if there were such correlations between specific mantras and specific individuals, any one of the thousands of teachers who introduce the novices to the secret could hardly know enough about the individuality of the new customer to make the right choice.) The idea of the custom-made mantra is the basis for selling it for a not-inconsiderable sum to the newcomer. "The personal wishes of the individual are taken into account and the *possibility of this fulfilment is confirmed* by the teacher."[2] What a promise! Any wish can be fulfilled, if only one practices T.M.

After having heard two introductory lectures, the novice has an interview with the teacher; then, with a little ceremony, he receives his personal mantra and is instructed never to say it aloud to himself or to anyone else. He has to sign a statement that he will never teach the method to others (obviously to keep the monopoly intact). The new adherent has a right to be checked every year about his progress by the teacher who introduced him, although, as I understand it, this is usually a brief routine procedure.

The movement has now many hundreds of thousands of practicing adherents, mainly in the United States but increasingly also in a number of European countries. The promise that T.M. holds out is, aside from the fulfillment of any personal wish, that the practice does not require any effort, yet it is the basis for successful, meaningful behavior. Success and inner growth go together, Caesar and God are reconciled, the more you grow spiritually the more successful you will also be in business. Indeed, the movement itself—its advertising, its vague and often meaningless language, its references to *some* respectable ideas, the cult of a smiling leader—has adopted all the features of big business.

The existence and popularity of the movement are as little

---

2. *Transcendental Meditation* (Maharishi International University Press, March 1974; emphasis added).

surprising as that of certain patent medicines. What is surprising is that among its adherents and practitioners are, as I know from personal experience, people of unquestionable integrity, high intelligence, and superior psychological insight. I must admit that I am puzzled by the fact. To be sure, their positive reaction is due to the relaxing and energizing effect of the meditation exercises. But what is so puzzling is that they are not repelled by the unclear language, the crude P.R. spirit, the exaggerated promises, the commercialization of the salvation business—and why they retain their connection with T.M. rather than choose another, nonmystifying technique such as one of those mentioned above. Has the spirit of big business and its selling methods already made such inroads that one must also accept them in the field of individual spiritual development?

In spite of the favorable effect of mantra meditation, it does, in my opinion, damage to the supporter. In order to appreciate this damage one must go beyond the isolated act of mantra meditation and see the entire fabric of which it is a part: One supports an idolatrous cult and thus decreases one's independence, one supports the dehumanizing feature of our culture—the commercialization of all values—as well as the spirit of P.R. falsehoods, the no-effort doctrine, and the perversion of traditional values such as self-knowledge, joy, well-being—by clever packaging. As a result, one's mind becomes confused and filled with new illusions in addition to those that exist already and should be gotten rid of.

There is another danger in movements like T.M. It is used by many people who are genuinely eager to achieve an inner change and to find a new meaning to life, and by its phraseology T.M. supports such wishes. But it is in fact at best only a method for relaxation, to be compared to Hatha Yoga or the honest Autogenic Training by the late Prof. I. H. Schultz, which achieved states of refreshing and energizing relaxation in many people. Such relaxation, while desirable, has nothing to do with a fundamental human change from egocentricity to inner freedom. Admittedly, it is useful for a vain and egocentric person just as it is for a person who has dropped much of his having structure, but by pretending that it is more than momentary relaxation, T.M. blocks the way for many who would seek a real path of liberation did they not believe they had found it in Transcendental Meditation.

Lately the movement has sought also to attract and incorporate those who have an interest not only in themselves but in mankind. The Maharishi announced a "World Plan" on January 8, 1972, after seven days of silence, to two-thousand new teachers of the "Science of Creative Intelligence" on the island of Mallorca. This World Plan is to be fulfilled by the construction of 3,500 "World Plan Centers," each center for one million people. Each will educate one-thousand teachers of the Science of Creative Intelligence, so that eventually every one-thousand people in every part of the world will be provided with a teacher. The World Plan has seven aims, among them: "to improve the achievements of governments" and "to abolish the old problems of crime and of all behavior that results in misfortune." For the realization of the seven goals there exist seven courses. Summarizing his aim, the Maharishi stated: "We shall consider ourselves as successful only then, when the problems of today's world are essentially diminished and eventually abolished and when the educational authorities of every country will be able to bring up fully developed citizens."[3]

Do these plans for the salvation of the world need any comment to prove their lack of any thought, which goes beyond vulgar selling methods?

The success of T.M. has given rise to similar ventures. One such enterprise was described in *Newsweek* (February 17, 1975). Its inventor, born Jack Rosenberg, now Werner (from Wernherr von Braun) Erhard (from the former German chancellor Ludwig Erhard), has founded Erhard Seminar Training (EST). In EST he packaged "his" experience with Yoga, Zen, sensitivity training, and encounter therapy into a new unit that is sold for 250 dollars in two weekend sessions. According to the 1975 report, already six-thousand salvation seekers had been processed, with

---

3. Ibid.

a large profit for EST. This is very little compared with T.M., yet it shows that by now not only an Indian but a former personal-motivation expert from a Philadelphia suburb can break into the business.

*   *   *

I have devoted so much space to these movements because I think there is an important lesson to be learned. The basis for any approach to self-transformation is an ever-increasing aware-ness of reality and the shedding of illusions. Illusions contami-nate even the most wonderful-sounding teaching to make it poisonous. I am not referring here to possible errors in the teach-ing. The Buddha's teachings are not contaminated because one does not believe that transmigration exists, nor is the biblical text contaminated because it contrasts with the more realistic knowledge of the history of the earth and the evolution of man. There are, however, intrinsic untruths and deceptions that do contaminate teaching, such as announcing that great results can be achieved without effort, or that the craving for fame can go together with egolessness, or that methods of mass suggestion are compatible with independence.

To be naïve and easily deceived is impermissible, today more than ever, when the prevailing untruths may lead to a catastrophe because they blind people to real dangers and real possibilities.

The "realists" believe, of those who strive for kindness, that these latter mean well but that they are ingenuous, full of illu-sions—briefly, fools. And they are not entirely wrong. Many of those who abhor violence, hate, and selfishness *are* naïve. They need their belief in everybody's innate "goodness" in order to sustain that belief. Their faith is not strong enough to believe in the fertile possibilities of man without shutting their eyes to the ugliness and viciousness of individuals and groups. As long as they do so, their attempts to achieve an optimum of well-being must fail; any intense disappointment will convince them that they were wrong or will drive them into a depression, because they do not then know what to believe.

Faith in life, in oneself, in others must be built on the hard

rock of realism; that is to say, on the capacity to see evil where
it is, to see swindle, destructiveness, and selfishness not only
when they are obvious but in their many disguises and rationalizations. Indeed, faith, love, and hope must go together with
such a passion for seeing reality in all its nakedness that the
outsider would be prone to call the attitude "cynicism." And
cynical it is, when we mean by it the refusal to be taken in by
the sweet and plausible lies that cover almost everything that is
said and believed. But *this* kind of "cynicism" is not cynicism; it
is uncompromisingly critical, a refusal to play the game in a
system of deception. Meister Eckhart expressed this briefly and
succinctly when he said of the "simple one" (whom Jesus taught):
"He does not deceive *but he is also not deceived*."[4]

Indeed, neither the Buddha, nor the Prophets, nor Jesus, nor
Eckhart, nor Spinoza, nor Marx, nor Schweitzer were "softies."
On the contrary, they were hardheaded realists and most of them
were persecuted and maligned not because they preached virtue
but because they spoke truth. They did not respect power, titles,
or fame, and they knew that the emperor was naked; and they
knew that power can kill the "truth-sayers."

3. Trivial Talk

Among the obstacles to learning the art of being, one other is:
indulging in *trivial talk*.

What is trivial? Literally it means "commonplace" (from Lat.
tri-via = the point where three roads meet); it usually denotes
shallow, humdrum, lacking ability or moral qualities. One might
also define "trivial" as an attitude that is concerned only with the
surface of things, not with their causes or the deeper layers; as
an attitude that does not distinguish between what is essential
and what is unessential, or one that is prone to reverse the two
qualities. We may say, in addition, that triviality results from

---

4. Sermon XXX, "Christ Sat in the Temple and Taught," *The Works of Master
Eckhart,* tr. Evans (emphasis added).

unaliveness, unresponsiveness, deadness, or from any concern that is not related to the central task of man: to be fully born. In this latter sense the Buddha has defined trivial talk. He said:

> If the mind of a monk inclines to talking, he should think thus: "I shall not engage in the low kind of talk that is vulgar, worldly and unprofitable; that does not lead to detachment, dispassion-ateness, cessation, tranquility, direct knowledge, enlightenment, Nirvana; namely talk about kings, thieves, ministers, armies, fam-ine and war; about eating, drinking, clothing and lodgings; about garlands, perfumes, relatives, vehicles, villages, towns, cities and countries; about women and wine, the gossip of the street and the well, talk about ancestors, about various trifles, tales about the origins of the world and the sea, talk about things being so or otherwise, and similar matters." Thus he has clear compre-hension.
>
> "But talk that is helpful for leading the austere life, useful for mental clarity, that leads to complete detachment, dispassion-ateness, cessation, tranquility, direct knowledge, enlightenment and Nibbana; that is talk on frugality, contentedness, solitude, seclusion, application of energy, virtue, concentration, wisdom, deliverance and on the knowledge and vision bestowed by deliver-ance—in such talk shall I engage." Thus he has clear compre-hension.[1]

Some of the examples cited for trivial conversation may not appear trivial to a non-Buddhist, such as the question of the origin of the world, or perhaps even a Buddhist might say that talk about famine, if serious and with the intention to help, was never meant to be trivial by the Buddha. However this may be, the whole list, in its bold summation of topics some of which are sacred to some and dear to many, is very impressive because it conveys the flavor of banality. How many billions of conversa-tions have taken place in these last years about inflation, Viet-nam, the Near East, Watergate, elections, etc., and how rarely do these conversations go beyond the obvious—the strict partisan

---

1. Mayshima-Nikaya, 122, quoted in Nyanaponika Thera, *The Heart of Bud-dhist Meditation* (New York: Samuel Weiser, 1973), p. 172.

viewpoint—and penetrate to the roots and causes of the phenomena that are discussed. One is prone to believe that most people need wars, crimes, scandals, and even illness in order to have something to talk about, that is in order to have a reason to communicate with each other even though on the level of triviality. Indeed, when human beings are transformed into commodities, what can their conversation be but trivial? Would commodities on the market, if they could speak, not talk about the customers, the behavior of the sales personnel, their own hopes of fetching a high price and their disappointment when it became clear that they would not be sold?

Perhaps most trivial talk is a need to talk about oneself; hence, the never-ending subject of health and sickness, children, travel, successes, what one did, and the innumerable daily things that *seem* to be important. Since one cannot talk about oneself all the time without being thought a bore, one must exchange the privilege by a readiness to listen to others talking about themselves. Private social meetings between individuals (and often, also, meetings of all kinds of associations and groups) are little markets where one exchanges one's need to talk about oneself and one's desire to be listened to for the need of others who seek the same opportunity. Most people respect this arrangement of exchange; those who don't, and want to talk more about themselves than they are willing to listen, are "cheaters," and they are resented and have to choose inferior company in order to be tolerated.

One can hardly overestimate people's need to talk about themselves and to be listened to. If this need were present only in highly narcissistic people, who are filled only with themselves, it would be easy to understand. But it exists in the average person for reasons that are inherent in our culture. Modern man is a mass man, he is highly "socialized," but he is very lonely. David Riesman has expressed this phenomenon strikingly in the title of his 1961 book *The Lonely Crowd* (New York: Free Press). Modern man is alienated from others and confronted with a dilemma: He is afraid of close contact with another and equally afraid to be alone and have no contact. It is the function of trivial conversation to answer the question "How do I remain alone without being lonely?"

Talking becomes an addiction. "As long as I talk, I know I exist; that I am not nobody, that I have a past, that I have a job, I have a family. And by talking about all this I affirm myself. However, I need someone to listen; if I were only talking to myself I would go crazy." The listener produces the illusion of a dialogue, when in reality there is only a monologue.

Bad company, on the other hand, is not only the company of merely trivial people but of evil, sadistic, destructive life-hostile people. But why, one might ask, is there a danger in the company of bad people, unless they try to harm one in one form or another?

In order to answer this question it is necessary to recognize a law in human relations: *There is no contact between human beings that does not affect both of them.* No meeting between two people, no conversation between them, except perhaps the most casual one, leaves either one of them unchanged—even though the change may be so minimal as to be unrecognizable except by its cumulative effect when such meetings are frequent.

Even a casual meeting *can* have a considerable impact. Who has not once been touched in his life by the kindness in a face of a person whom he saw only for a minute and never talked to? Who has not experienced the horror that a truly evil face produced in him, even being exposed to it for only a moment? Many will remember such faces and the effects they had on them for many years, or for all their lives. Who, after being with a certain person, has not felt cheered up, more alive, in a better mood, or in some cases even possessing new courage and new insights, even though the content of the conversation would not account for this change; on the other hand, many people have had the experience, after being with certain others, of being depressed, tired, hopeless, yet unable to find the *content* of the conversation responsible for the reaction. I am not speaking here of the influence of persons with whom somebody is in love, admires, is afraid of, etc; obviously *they* can have a strong influence by what they say or how they behave toward a person who is under their spell. What I am talking about is the influence of persons on those who are not bound to them in special ways.

All these considerations lead to the conclusion that it is desirable to avoid trivial and evil company altogether, unless one can assert oneself fully and thus make the other doubt his own position.

Inasmuch as one cannot avoid bad company, one should not be deceived: One should see the insincerity behind the mask of friendliness, the destructiveness behind the mask of eternal complaints about unhappiness, the narcissism behind the charm. One should also not act as if he or she were taken in by the other's deceptive appearance—in order to avoid being forced into a certain dishonesty oneself. One need not speak to them about what one sees, but one should not attempt to convince them that one is blind. The great twelfth-century Jewish philosopher Moses Maimonides, recognizing the effect of bad company, made the drastic proposal: "If you live in a country whose inhabitants are evil, avoid their company. If they try to force you to associate with them, leave the country, even if it means going to the desert."

If other people do not understand our behavior—so what? Their request that we must only do what they understand is an attempt to dictate to us. If this is being "asocial" or "irrational" in their eyes, so be it. Mostly they resent our freedom and our courage to be ourselves. We owe nobody an explanation or an accounting, as long as our acts do not hurt or infringe on them. How many lives have been ruined by this need to "explain," which usually implies that the explanation be "understood," i.e., approved. Let your deeds be judged, and from your deeds your real intentions, but know that a free person owes an explanation only to himself—to his reason and his conscience—and to the few who may have a justified claim for explanation.

4. "No Effort, No Pain"

Another barrier to learning the art of being is the "no-effort, no-pain" doctrine. People are convinced that everything, even the most difficult tasks, should be mastered without or with only little effort. This doctrine is so popular that it scarcely requires a lengthy explanation.

Take our entire method of education. We persuade our young people, we actually beg them, to get an education. In the name of "self-expression," "anti-achievement," "freedom," we make every course as easy and pleasant as possible. The only exceptions are the natural sciences, where real achievement is intended and where one cannot master the subject in "easy lessons." But in the social sciences, art, and literature courses, and in elementary and high schools, the same tendency is present. Make it easy and take it easy! The professor who insists on hard work is called "authoritarian," or old-fashioned.

The causes for this trend today are not difficult to discover. The increasing need for technicians, for half-educated people who work in service industries, from clerks to minor executives, requires people with a smattering of knowledge as our colleges provide it. Second, our whole social system rests upon the fictitious belief that nobody is forced to do what he does, but that he likes to do it. This replacement of overt by anonymous authority finds its expression in all areas of life: Force is camouflaged by consent; the consent is brought about by methods of mass suggestion. As a consequence, study too should be felt as pleasant, not enforced, and all the more so in fields in which the need for serious knowledge is minimal.

The idea of effortless learning has still another root: Technical progress has indeed diminished the amount of physical energy necessary for the production of goods. In the first industrial revolution, animal and human physical energy were replaced by the mechanical energy of the machine. In the second industrial revolution, thinking and memorizing are replaced by machines up to the large computers. This liberation from hard work is experienced as the greatest gift of modern "progress." And it *is* a gift—provided that the human energy thus liberated be applied to other, more elevated and creative tasks. However, this has not been the case. The liberation from the machine has resulted in the ideal of absolute laziness, of the horror of making any real effort. The *good* life is the *effortless* life; the necessity to make stong efforts is, as it were, considered to be a medieval remnant, and one makes strong efforts only if one is really forced to do so, not voluntarily. You take your car to the grocery store two blocks away in order to avoid the "effort" of walking; the clerk in the store punches three figures on the adding machine to save the mental effort of adding.

Related to the no-effort doctrine is the no-pain doctrine. This, too, has a phobic quality: to avoid under all circumstances pain and suffering, physically and, particularly, mentally. The era of modern progress claims to lead man into the promised land of painless existence. In fact, people develop a kind of chronic phobia of pain. Pain is referred to here in the broadest sense of the word, not merely physical and mental pain. It is also painful to practice musical scales for hours every day, to study a subject that is not interesting yet is necessary for acquiring the knowledge one is interested in; it is painful to sit and study when one would like to meet his girlfriend, or just walk, or have fun with friends. These are indeed small pains. Regretfully, one must be willing to accept them cheerfully and without fretting if one wants to learn what is essential, wants to correct whatever is wrong in one's hierarchy. As far as more severe suffering is concerned, it must indeed be said that to be happy is only the lot of a few, to suffer is the lot of all men. Solidarity among men has one of its strongest foundations in the experience of sharing one's own suffering with the suffering of all.

5. "Antiauthoritarianism"

Another obstacle to being is the phobia against anything that is considered *authoritarian*, that is to say, "forced" upon the individual and requiring discipline. This phobia is consciously conceived as desire for freedom, the complete freedom to decide. (Jean-Paul Sartre in his concept of freedom has given the philosophical rationalization for this ideal.) It has many roots. First of all, there is a socio-economic root. Capitalist economy is based on the principle of freedom, to sell and to buy without interference or restriction, the freedom to act without any restricting moral or political principles—except those explicitly codified by law, which on the whole tend to prevent willful damage to others. But even though bourgeois freedom had largely economic roots, we cannot understand the passionate character of the wish for liberty unless we take into account that this wish was also rooted in a powerful existential passion: The need to be oneself and not a means to be used for the purposes of others.

This existential desire for liberty slowly was repressed, however; in the desire to protect one's property, the genuine wish for freedom became a mere ideology. And yet, a seemingly paradoxical development set in in the last decades. Authoritarianism decreased considerably in the Western democracies, yet with it decreased, too, the *factual* freedom of the individual. What changed was not the *fact* of dependency but its *form*. In the nineteenth century those who ruled exercised overt, direct authority: kings, governments, priests, bosses, parents, teachers. With changing methods of production, particularly the increasing role of machines, and with the change from the idea of hard work and saving to the ideal of consumption ("happiness"), overt personal obedience to a *person* was substituted by submission to the *organization:* the endless belt, the giant enterprises, governments which persuaded the individual that he was free, that everything was done in his interests, that he, the public, was the real boss. Yet precisely because of the gigantic power and size of the bureaucracy of the state, army, industry, the replacement of personal bosses by impersonal bureaucracies, the individual became more powerless than he was, even before—but he is not aware of his powerlessness.

In order to defend himself against such an individually and socially disturbing awareness, he has now built up an ideal of absolute, unrestricted "personal" freedom. One manifestation of this has been the establishment of sexual freedom. Both the young and many of their middle-aged parents have tried to realize this ideal of freedom by rejecting any restrictions in the sphere of sexual relations. To be sure, this was partly a very wholesome process. After two-thousand years of religious defamation, sexual desire and satisfaction ceased to be considered sinful, and hence constant guilt feelings and thus a readiness to atone for that guilt by renewed submission were reduced. But even with due appreciation of the historical significance of the "sexual revolution," one should not ignore some other, less favorable "side effects" of that revolution. It tried to establish the freedom of *whim* instead of the freedom of *will*.

What is the difference? A whim is any desire that emerges spontaneously, without any structural connection with the whole personality and its goals. (In young children they form part of a normal pattern.) The desire itself—even the most fleeting or irrational one—today requires its fulfillment; to disregard it or even to postpone it is experienced as an infringement of one's freedom. If a man meets a woman accidentally, has a few free hours, is bored, he may easily consider the idea of sleeping with her. Once the idea has appeared on his mental screen he decides to act accordingly, not necessarily because the woman attracts him particularly or because his sexual need is so intense, but because of the compulsive need to act out what even he has conceived as a wish. Or, say, a detached, lonely adolescent, who walks along the street, suddenly has the thought that it would be exciting to stab the young nurse whom he passes—and he stabs her to death. These are not merely a few instances in which people have followed whims. That the first act is lovemaking and the second is killing is of course a significant difference. But what they have in common is the character of a whim. Examples between these extremes abound, and anyone can find them for himself.

The general criterion of a whim is that it responds to the question "Why not?" and not to the question "Why?" I am sure that anyone who observes behavior minutely has discovered with what extraordinary frequency people, when asked whether they would like to do this or that, begin their answer with "Why not?" This "Why not?" implies that one does something simply because there is no reason against doing it, not because there is a reason *for* it; it implies that it is a whim but not a manifestation of the will. Following a whim is, in fact, the result of deep inner passivity blended with a wish to avoid boredom. Will is based on activity, whim on passivity.

The most significant place in which the fiction of personal freedom is acted out is the area of consumption. The customer is the king of the supermarket and the automobile market. Many brands of each commodity vie for his favor. They have tried to entice him for months on the television screen, and when he buys he seems to be like a powerful man who, in full freedom, makes his choices between soap powder A, B, and C—all of which beg for his vote as political candidates do before election day. The customer-king is not aware that he has no influence on what is offered him, and that the alleged choice is no "choice" since the different brands are essentially the same, sometimes even manufactured by the same corporation.

It is possible to formulate a general psychological law: The greater the sense of powerlessness and the greater the lack of authentic will, the more grows either submission or an obsessional desire for satisfaction of one's whims and the insistence on arbitrariness.

To sum up: The chief rationalization for the obsession of arbitrariness is the concept of antiauthoritarianism. To be sure, the fight against authoritarianism was and still is of great positive significance. But antiauthoritarianism can—and has—become a rationalization for narcissistic self-indulgence, for a childlike sybaritic life of unimpaired pleasure, in which according to Herbert Marcuse even the primacy of *genital* sexuality is authoritarian, because it restricts the freedom of pregenital—i.e., anal—perversions. Finally, the fear of authoritarianism serves to rationalize a kind of madness, a desire to escape from reality. Reality imposes its law on man, laws that he can only escape in dreams or in states of trance—or in insanity.

PART III

6. "To Will One Thing"

The first condition for more than mediocre achievement in any field, including that of the art of living, is to *will one thing*.[1] To will one thing presupposes having made a decision, having committed oneself to one goal. It means that the whole person is geared and devoted to the one thing he has decided on, that all his energies flow in the direction of this chosen goal.

Where energies are split in different directions, an aim is not only striven for with diminished energy, but the split of energies has the effect of weakening them in both directions by the constant conflicts that are engendered.

An obsessional neurosis is a case in point. The will of a person who is doubting whether he should do one thing or its opposite, whose attitude toward the most important people in his life is one of extreme ambivalence, may become completely paralyzed in making any decisions and or eventually in acting altogether. In the 'normal' case, where the aims are not so rigidly opposed, a smaller amount of energy is wasted; nevertheless, the capacity to reach any goal is greatly reduced. It actually does not matter what the goal is—material or spiritual, moral or immoral. A bank robber needs to will one thing just as much as a scientist or a violinist, provided that they want to do what they're doing excellently or even competently. Halfheartedness leads one to prison, the others to becoming an unproductive and bored college professor or a member of a second-class orchestra, respec-

---

1. Cf. S. Kierkegaard's *Purity of the Heart and to Will One Thing: Spiritual Preparation for the Office of Confession* (New York: Harper and Brothers, 1938).

31

tively. Of course, if only amateur status is aspired to, matters are different: the thief will probably get into trouble, the scientist will likely feel frustrated, while the amateur violinist will thoroughly enjoy his activity for its intrinsic value, provided he does not expect to achieve excellence.

It is easy to observe the frequency of unresolved contradictions of goals within people. In part they are derived from a split in our culture, which provides its members with opposite sets of norms: those of Christian charity and altruism and those of bourgeois indifference and selfishness. While in practice the norm of selfishness is generally adopted, quite a few people are nevertheless still influenced by the old norms, yet not strongly enough to lead them to a different conduct of life.

In contemporary industrial society the opportunities for doing things wholeheartedly are greatly reduced. Indeed, if the worker on the endless belt, the bureaucrat filing papers, the street cleaner, or the man selling stamps behind the post-office window tried to do this with a whole heart and a unified will, he would be in danger of becoming crazy. Thus, he tries to detach himself as much as he can from that work and occupy his mind with all sorts of thoughts, daydreams, or—with nothing. But there are still a number of occupations that permit the development of excellence. To name a few: those of a scientist, a physician, an artist, even of a secretary who has interesting work to do, or the work of a nurse, a bus driver, an editor, a pilot, a carpenter. The increasing mechanization and routinization of work, however, will reduce these possibilities more and more.

To begin with, even manual and clerical work need not be automatized and routinized as it is now. As a number of recent experiments show, one can reduce the monotony of work and create the possibility of a certain degree of interest and skill by reversing the process of overspecialization and changing the methods of production in such a way that the worker decides on his method of operating and thus ceases to be narrowed down to the repetition of one or two mechanical movements. However, in any kind of industrial mass production there are limitations to the extent to which work will permit the development of interest and the striving for excellence.

The matter is quite different where we do not speak of the *technical* aspect of work but of its *social* aspect. This is more obvious today, when nearly all work is teamwork, from the work in an automobile plant to that in a research institute. Everyone finds himself in a net of interpersonal relations and is part of it, in various ways and to varying degrees. The social situation in which I live is part of my own life; it affects me as I affect it. If the blue- and white-collar workers in an industrial enterprise or the nurses and employees in the hospital once they cease to be "employed" participated in managing the institutions by themselves, if they could build a community together with all who work in the same institution, they would have a task set before them that can achieve excellence by the rationality of organization and the quality of human relations. In such productive work each would also work productively on his own life.[2]

Aside from the place of work as a social organization, the optimal organization of society as a whole gives everyone the possibility to contribute with his whole heart. However, to achieve this would require that society and its political representative, the state, ceased to be powers that stood over and against the citizen, but that they are the product of his work. At the present stage of alienation this is quite impossible; in a humanized society, aside from his own life, society itself becomes man's most important work fact—and the ends of both coincide.

7. To Be Awake

Today there is much talk among seekers of new paths about altering and widening the state of consciousness. One usually means by this something like seeing the world in a new light,

---

2. Cf. the lengthier discussion of this point in E. Fromm, *The Sane Society* (New York: Rinehart & Co., 1955).

especially in a physical sense, with colors and forms appearing with greater intensity and in entirely original forms. Various means are recommended to reach this state of altered consciousness, primarily the psycho-drugs of various intensities and self-induced states of trance. No one can deny that such states of altered consciousness can occur; but few people who are so enthusiastic about them seem to raise the question why anyone would want to alter his consciousness, when, in his normal state of being, he has not even reached the state of normally developed consciousness. The fact is, most of those who are so eager to reach states of altered consciousness do not have more developed states of consciousness than their fellow men who only drink coffee, liquor, and smoke cigarettes. Binges of widened consciousness are escapes from a narrow consciousness, and after the "trip" they are no different from what they were before and from how their fellow men have been all the time: Half-awake people.

This term "half awake" needs some explanation, especially since I introduce it to denote the customary state of mind in most people. We believe we are on solid ground if we distinguish between sleeping and being awake, and up to a certain extent we are. There are definite physiological—i.e., chemical and electrical—differences between the two states. From a psycho-biological standpoint the differences can be thus described: In the state of awakeness the total person fulfills the function of providing food and shelter and other necessities of life and of protecting himself against dangers, mainly by fighting or running away—or, in man, by negotiating a compromise that avoids both equally dangerous alternatives. In the state of sleep man is freed from the function of having to make efforts for survival; he does not need to work, and only emergency signals such as unusual noises wake him up for self-defense. He is turned inward and is capable of formulating messages to himself, creating, directing, and acting out plays in which he expresses his wishes, his fears, and his deepest insights into himself and others—insights made possible by the fact that he is not drugged by the voices of common sense and illusions that intrude on him while he is awake.[1]

In fact, paradoxically, we are more awake when we are asleep than when we are not. Our dreams often testify to our creative activity, our daydreams to our mental laziness. However, both the sleeping state and the waking state are not two undifferentiated entities. Within each state are many substates: from light to deep sleep—states in which we dream (recognizable by an observer because our eyes move and technically called REM sleep) and states in which we do not dream.

It is also known that definite distinctions exist within the waking state; they have been studied by means of analyzing differing kinds of electric waves emitted by the brain. Although our scientific knowledge in this field is still rudimentary, empirical self-observation, however, can provide us with data that we have not yet obtained in a more exact way. Everybody recognizes differences in the state of alertness, openness, vigor of mind, as against states of a certain sluggishness or inattentiveness. At the same time, it is also a matter of general experience that these two states can follow each other very rapidly, so that the usual explanation of not having had enough sleep or "just being tired" can be excluded. It is interesting to analyze what factor changes the state of "tiredness" to that of intense alertness.

The most obvious example is that of the influence of people. The same man who was sitting in his office doing his routine work correctly yet listlessly, only sufficiently concentrated to do his work properly, leaves the office and meets a woman whom he is in love with. He is suddenly another man—alert, witty, attractive, full of life, energetic. One might say that from being half asleep he has become wide-awake. Or the opposite case: A married man, quite immersed in work that is interesting, may be very alert and awake; he comes home—and he may totally change. He may become bored, half drowsy, want to look at

---

1. Cf. a more detailed analysis in E. Fromm, *The Forgotten Language* (New York: Rinehart & Co., 1951).

television, to have a drink, hoping that these will stimulate him. When this fails to occur, some desultory conversation with his wife may follow, then more television, and a sigh of relief when the day is over—topped sometimes by a bit of tired sex. (This, of course, happens only in "tired marriages," where people have long ceased to be in love—if they ever were.)

Other motives also stimulate awakeness: a danger, a chance to win, or destroy, or to conquer, or to satisfy any of the passions that are able to stimulate a person. One could say, justifiedly: "Tell me what wakes you up and I'll tell you who you are."

It would be a mistake, though, to assume that the *quality* of being fully awake is independent of the stimuli that produce this result. The man brought to full awakeness by awareness of a danger will be mainly alert to all factors pertaining to this threat; the man brought to life by the chance of gaining in gambling may remain quite unaware of his wife's anguish about his addiction to it. To put it more generally, we become alert in the way and to the degree with which a vitally necessary task (such as working or defending one's vital interests) or a passionate goal (such as the quest for money) requires it. Different from this partial and, as it were, pragmatic alertness is a state of total awakeness. In this state one is not only aware of that which one needs to be aware of in order to survive or to satisfy passionate goals, one is aware of oneself and of the world (people and nature) around one. One sees, not opaquely but clearly, the surface together with its roots. The world becomes fully real; every detail and the details in their configuration and structure become a meaningful unit. It feels as if a veil that had been in front of our eyes permanently—without our recognizing it was there—and had suddenly dropped away.

This is an example of awakeness, known to everybody: We have seen the face of a person many times, he may be a relative, a friend, an acquaintance, a companion at work. One day, for reasons that we often do not understand, we suddenly see his face in a completely new manner. It is as if it has assumed a new dimension. It has come fully to life for us (even in its un-aliveness, if this be the case). We see with an extraordinary clarity, distinctness, reality. We see in it the man, not his "problems," his past, nothing that leads us to theoretical considerations, just him, in his "suchness." He may be evil or kind, strong or weak, brutal or delicate (or any blend of these factors), he has become *he* for us and his face remains in our mind. We can never think of him in the bland, blurred, distant way he had appeared to us before. It is of course not necessarily the face that has become so expressive. For quite a few people the hand, the shape of the body, the gestures and movements are of equal significance, or even more so.

Two people look at each other and are aware of each other. They see each other in their unique suchness, there is no barrier, no fog; they see in a state of intense awakeness; in this process of direct, unimpeded awareness, they do not *think* about each other, they do not raise psychological questions, do not ask how the person has become what he is, how he will develop, whether he is good or evil; they are just *aware*. Later on, indeed they may *think* of each other; they may analyze, evaluate, clarify—but if they thought while they are aware, the awareness would suffer.

8. To Be Aware

Generally the words "to be aware," "to know," "to be conscious of" are considered to be synonymous. Yet the etymological roots of "aware" point to a difference from the two other words; the root of *aware* (as the German *gewahr*) has in the English and German history of the word the meaning "attention" or "mindfulness" (German *Aufmerksamkeit*). It is usually construed as to be or to become aware of something. This means more than simple consciousness or knowledge; it has the meaning of discovering something that was not quite obvious, or was even not expected. In other words, awareness is knowing or consciousness in a state of close attention.

Let us consider the different meanings of awareness. Awareness can refer to one's body or to one's psychic state (i.e., one's feelings and one's mood).

A simple example of bodily awareness is to become aware of one's breathing. Of course, we know that we are breathing, but this is an intellectual knowledge that can be proven by our observing the fact of breathing, of inhaling and exhaling, or the movement of our abdomen. But this knowledge that we breathe is something quite different from the awareness of the act of breathing. Anybody can notice the difference by making a simple experiment. One sits down in a relaxed—that is, neither slouching nor rigid—posture, closes one's eyes, tries to think of nothing and just feel one's breathing. This is by no means as easy as it sounds, because many thoughts will intrude and one will notice, especially in the beginning, that after a few seconds one stopped being aware of one's breathing and began to think of many often irrelevant things. To the degree to which one succeeds in concentrating on one's breathing, one is aware of the process of breathing. Without trying to force it or to control it, without any purpose or goal at all, one gives oneself to the act of breathing. One will discover that this awareness of breathing is something quite different from thinking about one's breathing. In fact, the two modes exclude each other. As soon as I think *about* my breathing, I cannot be aware of the act of breathing.

Another example,[1] also simple for anyone to try, is the following: Again one assumes the relaxed position and closes one's eyes. The hands are resting on one's upper legs (the posture one can see in the statues of the famous Abu Simbel sitting Pharaohs). One decides to raise one arm up to a forty-five-degree angle. When we do this normally, with open eyes, our nervous system gives a signal to the corresponding muscles and we raise the arm. We do it immediately, we see the effect; the order is fulfilled and we can give the order to drop it to its original position. Have we experienced the movement of the arm? Hardly: The arm is an instrument, and there is little difference from our pushing a button that would elevate an artificial arm.

---

1. This example is taken from the method of "sensory awareness" that is described (in the form applied by Charlotte Selver) by Charles Brooks in *Sensory Awareness: The Rediscovery of Experiencing* (New York: Viking, 1974).

What matters is the effect, not the process. If, in contrast to the usual method, we want to concentrate on the experience of the movement, we must try to forget the end and move the arm with such slowness that we begin to feel how it moves—from the subtle raising of the palm from the rest, to the moment when it is "airborne," then further and further when it eventually has arrived at more or less the planned height, and then as we move it down again until it comes to a full rest. Anybody who does this little exercise will notice that he experiences the moving arm, and not that he is a witness to "movement." He will also recognize that he is so concentrating on being aware of the movement that he does not think or reflect about it; he may think or reflect *about* it before or afterward, but in the process of becoming aware thinking is excluded.

The same principle exists in the "art of moving" (taught by Katya Delakova) and in an old Chinese traditional sequence of movements, the T'ai Chi Chuan. (The latter is a particularly recommendable exercise because it combines elements of "sensory awareness" with a state of concentrated meditation.)[2]

The same difference between awareness and thinking exists also with regard to the awareness of our feelings and moods. If I am aware of feeling joy, love, sadness, fear, or hate, this means that I feel and that the feeling is not repressed; it does not mean I think or *reflect about* my feeling. It would also be correct to say "I am conscious" of what I feel; *conscious* comes from the Latin root *con* = with + *scire* = to know; i.e., participating in knowledge, or "with mental faculties awake." To be conscious contains an active element similar to "to be aware of." The German equivalent, *Bewusstsein,* is even more expressive; it is bewusstes Sein = conscious being. (Until the eighteenth century it is used in philosophical language in two words: "bewusst Sein.")

Thus far, I have discussed awareness of what is not hidden. A different kind of awareness is that of becoming aware of what is

---

2. I am indebted to Charlotte Selver for her teaching of "sensory awareness" in the 1940s and to Katya Delakova for her teaching of the "art of moving" and especially of the T'ai Chi Chuan in the last ten years.

hidden. This becoming aware of what is hidden is the same as becoming conscious of what is unconscious (repressed), or to *make* conscious what is repressed, since in general it requires an active effort if something unconscious is to become conscious. We could also call the same process *revealing* or *uncovering awareness*.

The two most far-reaching, eye-opening critical theories at the beginning of the latest phase of industrial society were those of Marx and of Freud.[3] Marx showed the moving powers and the conflicts in the social-historical process, Freud aimed at the critical uncovering of the inner conflicts. Both worked for the liberation of man, even though Marx's concept was more comprehensive and less time-bound than Freud's. Both theories also share the fate that they soon lost their most important quality, that of critical and thus liberating thought, and were transformed by most of their "faithful" adherents into ideologies, and their authors into idols.

The fact that Freud's and Marx's critical analyses can be considered to express the same idea in two different dimensions is based on a fundamental consideration.

Awareness refers not only to the uncovering of inner conflicts but equally to conflicts in social life that are negated and harmonized by ideologies (social rationalizations). Since the individual is a part of society and cannot be conceived of outside the social fabric, the illusions about social reality affect the clarity of his mind and thus also prevent him from liberating himself from the illusions about himself. The capacity to see and—equally so—blindness are not divisible. The critical faculty of the human mind is one: To believe one can be seeing internally but blind as far as the outside world is concerned is like saying that the light of a candle gives light only in one direction and not in all. The light of a candle is reason's capacity for critical, penetrating, uncovering thought.

---

3. Buddhism too was a critical theory, which, like Marxism, mobilized the activity of millions, just as Marx's theories did in the nineteenth century. (I am indebted to Z. Fišer for pointing out to me this parallel.)

Two questions must arise: Is the liberating effect of awareness possible, and if so how? Furthermore is awareness necessarily desirable?

There can be no doubt that it is possible. There are many examples throughout history for the fact that man is able to undo the chains of illusion and penetrate to the roots and thus to the causes of phenomena. I am referring here not only to the "great men," but to many ordinary people, who sometimes for unknown reasons shed the illusions obstructing their eyes and begin to see. More about this will be said in the later discussion of psychoanalysis.

One answer to the question why it is possible seems to lie in the following consideration: The strength of man's position in the world depends on the degree of adequacy of his perception of reality. The less adequate it is, the more disoriented and hence insecure he is and hence in need of idols to lean on and thus find security. The more adequate it is, the more can he stand on his own feet and have his center within himself. Man is like Antaeus, who charged himself with energy by touching Mother Earth, and who could be killed only when his enemy kept him long enough in the air.

The question of whether shedding one's blindness is desirable is more difficult to answer. There will be considerable agreement that it is desirable, provided the insight into the hidden conflicts leads to a constructive solution and hence to greater well-being. This is what Marx expected if the working class would become aware of its own conditions. If the working class would get rid of its illusions, it would build a society that would not require any illusions (and this *could* be done, because the historical conditions were ripe). Freud believed that the insight into the hidden conflicts between conscious and unconscious forces would result in the cure of neurosis.

But what if the conflict cannot be solved? Is man not better off to live with illusions than with a painful truth that does not help him to liberate himself in real life? If, as Marx and Freud believed, the teachings of religion were an illusion, was it a necessary one in order to make it possible for man to survive at all?

What would have happened to him if he had given up this illusion and experienced nothing but despair at seeing no chance for a more human social order and greater personal well-being? Or, if a sadistic, obsessional person recognized the roots of his suffering, and yet, for a number of possible reasons, knew also that he could not change, would he not be better off if he remained blind and continued to believe in his rationalizations?

Who will dare to answer these questions? At first glance, it would seem that the wish not to make anyone suffer unnecessarily should be a sufficient reason to plead in favor of not wanting to liberate him from his illusions. Yet I cannot help having some misgivings about this answer. Is this not the same as the question of whether one should tell a patient the truth about a terminal illness? Does one not deprive him of the last possibility to face his life, to gather all the inner force that he had not mobilized, and rise above fear to serenity and strength? This latter question has often been under discussion; it seems to me that the most concerned observers will refuse to choose, dogmatically, one or the other solution; they will agree that it depends on the personality of the dying person and that the judgment can be made only after one has tried to assess that person's inner actual and potential strength and to understand his deepest, often-unexpressed wish. It would seem to me inhuman to force upon him the truth in any dogmatic belief that it is necessarily "the best for him."

In matters of conflicts and illusions in general, a similar reasoning appears justified. In the first place, the question is in part purely abstract, and hence a wrong question; most individuals as well as social classes who cannot bear disillusionment without positive solutions will simply not listen to, understand, and certainly not agree with the disillusioning analysis, even if the critical thinker speaks with the voice of an angel. Examples in social and individual life of the strength of resistance abound and there is no need to cite any. But what about those whose resistance is not so massive? Are they necessarily better off keeping their illusions?

In order to answer this question we must remember that becoming aware of the truth has a liberating effect; it releases energy and de-fogs one's mind. As a result, one is more independent, has one's center in oneself, and is more alive. One may fully realize that nothing in reality can be changed, but one has succeeded in living and dying as a human person and not as a sheep. If avoidance of pain and maximal comfort are supreme values, then indeed illusions are preferable to the truth. If, on the other hand, we consider that every man, at any time in history, is born with the potential of being a full man and that, furthermore, with his death the one chance given to him is over, then indeed much can be said for the personal value of shedding illusions and thus attaining an optimum of personal fulfillment. In addition, the more seeing individuals will become, the more likely it is that they can produce changes—social and individual ones—at the earliest possible moment, rather than, as is often the case, waiting until the chances for change have disappeared because their mind, their courage, their will have become atrophied.

The conclusion from all these considerations is that the most important step in the art of being is everything that leads to and enhances our capacity for heightened awareness and, as far as the mind is concerned, for critical, questioning thinking. This is not primarily a question of intelligence, education, or age. It is essentially a matter of character; more specifically, of the degree of personal independence from irrational authorities and idols of all kinds that one has achieved.

How is this greater independence to be achieved? What can be said here is only this: Once one is aware of the crucial importance of non-submission (I mean here of inner non-submission and not necessarily of purely defiant, dogmatic disobedience), one will become very sensitive to the small signs of submission, one will look through the rationalization that justifies it, one will practice courage, and one will discover that once the problem and its central significance are recognized, one discovers by oneself many answers to the question. It is the same as it is with everything else: One discovers answers to problems only when one feels that they are burning and that it is a matter of life and death to solve them. If nothing is of burning interest, one's reason and one's critical faculty operate on a low level of activity; it appears then that one lacks the faculty to observe.

Another helpful attitude is one of deep distrust. Since most of what we hear is either plainly untrue, or half true and half distorted, and since most of what we read in the newspapers is distorted interpretations served as facts, it is by far the best plan to start out with radical skepticism and the assumption that most of what one hears is likely to be a lie or a distortion. If this sounds too grim and cynical, I might add that I do not mean this quite literally but that I want to emphasize that it is much more healthful than the opposite premise, namely, to believe that people say the truth until the opposite is proven.

My recommendation may sound perhaps less misanthropic if I stress that I spoke of the truth of statements, not about people who are liars. It would perhaps be simpler, although less bearable, if most people could be thus qualified, but the fact is, a majority of people whose statements are untrue or half true believe sincerely that they are speaking the truth, or at least persuade themselves of this while they are making their statements.

As for the practical steps to self-awareness, I shall discuss them later in the chapter on Pyschoanalysis and Self-Analysis. First, however, I want to discuss some other steps in the learning of the art of living.

9. To Concentrate

The capacity to concentrate has become a rarity in the life of cybernetic man. On the contrary, it seems as if he does everything to avoid concentration. He likes to do several things at the same time, such as listen to music, read, eat, talk with friends. A cartoon has expressed this trend quite succinctly: A man has installed a television on the wall above his bed, so that he could look at the screen while he was making love!

Indeed, television is a good teacher of non-concentration. By interruptions of a program for advertising, the audience becomes conditioned *not* to concentrate. Reading habits exhibit the same tendency. The fashion of editing and publishing anthologies accentuates this trend. Worse, one is offered fragments of thought by an author as a substitute for reading his book; thereby one does not need to concentrate in order to grasp a complex system of thoughts, but gets the "meat" in easy chunks that require far less concentration. Many students have the habit of never reading a whole book, even if there is no anthology or abridgment. The introduction, the conclusion, some pages that the professor has indicated—and one "knows" the author's thought, at least superficially and without need to concentrate.

How little concentration on a subject and on the other person occurs in conversations is surely known to anyone who observes average oral exchanges. When people are by themselves they also avoid concentrating on anything; they immediately pick up a newspaper or a magazine, which permits easy reading and demands no real concentration.

Concentration is such a rare phenomenon because one's will is not directed to one thing; nothing is worth the effort to concentrate on it, because no goal is pursued passionately. But there is more to it: People are afraid to concentrate because they are afraid of losing themselves if they are too absorbed in another person, in an idea, in an event. The less strong their self, the greater the fear of losing themselves in the act of concentration on the non-self. For the person with a dominant having orientation this fear of losing oneself is one of the main factors that operates against concentration. Finally, to concentrate requires inner activity, not busy-ness, and this activity is rare today when busy-ness is the key to success.

There is still another reason why people are afraid of concentrating: They think that concentrating is too strenuous an activity and that they would get tired quickly. In fact the opposite is true, as anyone can observe in oneself. Lack of concentration makes one tired, while concentration wakes one up. There is no mystery in this. In unconcentrated activity no energy is mobilized, since a low level of energy is sufficient to do the task. Mobilization of energy, which has a psychic as well as a physiological aspect, has the effect of making one feel alive.

The difficulty with concentrating is, in the last analysis, the outcome of the whole structure of the contemporary system of production and consumption. The more man's work is to service a machine or to act as that part of a machine that has not yet been devised in iron or steel, the less has he a chance to concentrate. The process of work is too monotonous to permit genuine concentration. The same holds true for consumption. The market offers as many different bits of amusement as possible, such a variety that it is neither necessary nor possible to concentrate on any one thing. Where would industry be if people began to concentrate on a few things rather than getting tired quickly of something and rushing out to buy new things that are exciting because they are new?

How does one learn to concentrate? The answer to this question must be either very brief or very long. For reasons of space, it must be brief.

As a first step, I suggest to practice how to be still. Concretely speaking, this means to sit still for, say, ten minutes, to do nothing, and as far as possible to think of nothing, but to be aware of what is going on in oneself. Anyone who thinks this is easy has never tried. One who tries finds immediately that it is quite difficult. He will notice that he is fidgety; that he moves his hand, his legs, his body. This becomes even more marked when he tries the classic sitting position we still see on the statues and pictures of the pharaohs: Legs not crossed but firmly planted in front of one, arms on an armrest or on the upper leg. But the position should be neither stiff as we learn it in old-fashioned military-style gymnastics nor slouching and lazy. It is something else: The body is in a harmonious position, it feels alive and comfortable in an active way. If one has learned this kind of sitting, one feels uncomfortable in an overstuffed chair, and comfortable sitting in a straight chair.

This practice of sitting is one step to learning concentration. It should be extended from 10 to 15 or 20 minutes and done regularly every day in the morning, and it is very recommendable to practice it at least for 5 to 10 minutes in the evening, and if possible once more during the day. After having achieved a certain amount of stillness—the effort may last from one to three months—it is to be recommended to add direct concentration exercises during or after the stillness. Practically speaking, this can be done in many ways. One may focus on a coin and concentrate completely on all its details, to the point where one sees it fully with closed eyes; or one may use any other object—a vase, a clock, a telephone, a flower, a leaf, a stone, or whatever one wishes to concentrate on. Or, instead, one may concentrate on a word.

For many months many other thoughts will pass through one's mind and disrupt the concentration. Here, as with everything living, force does not do any good; it does not help to try to force out tangential thoughts, to treat them as if they were enemies, and hence to feel defeated if one has not won the battle. They need to be treated gently, and that means one must be patient with oneself. (Impatience is usually the outcome of the intention to force.) Slowly, very slowly indeed, will intruding thoughts diminish in frequency and one will be better able to concentrate.

Another, even more formidable obstacle is that of getting sleepy and frequently one will find oneself on the verge of dozing off. This too one must take in one's stride. One may try again immediately, or take a few deep breaths and if the sleepiness persists one may stop and try again at a better time. To cope with these difficulties makes the learning of concentration so difficult because many, if not most, people become discouraged after a while. They may criticize themselves for their inability, or rationalize their failure by deciding that the whole method is no good anyway. Here, as in any act of learning, the capacity to tolerate failure is of crucial importance.

Machine production, where the object is spewed out by the machine, knows no failures, but it knows no excellence either. Production by machine has led to a peculiar illusion that the road to excellence is straight and pleasant; that the violin does not make scratching noises; that the study of a philosophical system does not leave one often puzzled and lost; that the perfect meal is produced after having once read the recipe in the cookbook.

Only if one knows that the road to concentration, as to any other achievement, necessarily brings with it failures, and disappointments, can one avoid the discouragement that is unavoidable in the process of learning to concentrate.

The simple exercises described above should be accompanied or followed by practicing concentration on thoughts and on feelings. For instance, one reads a book on a significant topic by an author who can be supposed to have something significant to say, and one can observe in what way one reads the book: Whether one becomes restless after an hour; whether one tries to skip pages; whether one rereads a page if it has not become quite clear at the first reading; whether one thinks about the author's argument, formulates responses or new ideas of one's own; whether one tries to understand what the author really means, rather than sticking to critiques of this or that point in order to refute the author; whether one wants to learn something new or have one's own views confirmed directly or indirectly by the faults of an opposing view.

These are some of the symptoms that help us to find out whether we read in a concentrated fashion. If we discover that we are not concentrated, we should practice concentration in reading by going to the essence of the author's thought, often at the expense of reading fewer books.

To concentrate on another person is essentially not different from concentrating on thoughts. I must leave it to the experience of each reader to gather material for the thesis that most of our personal relationships suffer from the complete absence of concentration. We tend to be very poor judges of character because we do not go much beyond grasping the surface of another's personality—i.e., what he says, how he behaves, what position he has, how he is dressed. In short, we observe the *persona,* the mask that he shows us, and we do not penetrate through this surface to lift the mask and see who the *person* is behind it. This we can only do if we concentrate on him. But it seems we are afraid to know anybody fully—including ourselves.

Individuality interferes with the smooth running of the process. Concentrated observation of one person forces us to respond with compassion, care, or, on the other hand, horror—all of which are unfavorable to the smooth functioning of a cybernetic society. We want distance, we want to know of each other just as much as is necessary to live together, to cooperate, to feel secure. Hence, knowledge of the surface is desirable, knowledge gained from concentration is disturbing.

There are other helpful forms of concentration, such as certain sports like tennis or mountain climbing, and games, such as chess; and there is playing an instrument or painting and sculpting. All these activities can be done in a concentrated or in an unconcentrated form. Primarily they are done in an unconcentrated form, and thus contribute nothing to learning concentration; whenever they are done in a concentrated form their mental effect is entirely different. But even without doing any of these things one can live continuously in a concentrated fashion. As we shall see later, the Buddhist concept of mindfulness means precisely a way of being in which one is fully concentrated on everything one is doing at any given moment, whether it is planting a seed or cleaning a room or eating. Or as a Zen master has said: "When I sleep I sleep, when I eat I eat. . . ."

10. To Meditate

From the practice of concentration a direct path leads to one of the basic preparations for learning the art of being: to meditate.

To begin with, one must distinguish between two different kinds of meditation: a) States of self-induced slight trance by the use of autosuggestive techniques, which can lead to mental and physical relaxation and make the practitioner feel refreshed, rested, and more energetic. An example of such methods is the "autogenous training" developed by the late Professor I. H. Schultz in Berlin. It has been practiced by many thousands of people and generally with good success.[1] Schultz never claimed

---

1. My wife and I studied with Professor Schultz, but without too much success because of an inner resistance to its autosuggestive character.

that the method served as anything other than mental relaxation. Since it is a method that one has to practice oneself, it is also not entirely passive, and does not make one dependent on the person of the teacher.

In contrast to autosuggestive forms of meditation, are those the main aim of which is to achieve a higher degree of non-attachment, of non-greed, and of non-illusion; briefly, those that serve to reach a higher level of being. In *Buddhist meditation* I have found a simple, unmystifying and non-suggestive form of meditation that has the aim of bringing one nearer to the Buddhist goal, that of the cessation of greed, hate, and ignorance. Fortunately we have an excellent description of Buddhist meditation by Nyanaponika Mahathera,[2] which I recommend to everybody who is seriously interested in learning this method of meditation.

The following remarks should indicate what the reader will find in the book. The aim of Buddhist meditation is *maximum awareness* of our bodily and mental processes. The author states that

the systematic cultivation of Right Mindfulness, as taught by the Buddha in his Discourse on *Satipatthana*[3] [mindfulness], still provides the most simple and direct, the most thorough and effective method for training and developing the mind for its daily tasks and problems as well as for its highest aim: the mind's own unshakable deliverance from Greed, Hatred and Delusion.

The teachings of the Buddha offer a great variety of methods of mental training and subjects of meditation, suited to the various individual needs, temperaments and capacities. Yet all these methods ultimately converge in the "Way of Mindfulness" called by the Master himself "the Only Way" (or: the Sole Way, *ekayano maggo*). The Way of Mindfulness may therefore rightly be called "the heart of Buddhist meditation" or even "the heart of the entire

2. Nyanaponika Mahathera, *The Heart of Buddhist Meditation* (New York: Samuel Weiser, 1973 [first published 1962 by Rider & Co., London]).

3. Cf. chapters 2–5 on Watchfulness in Moshe Chayim Lazetto, *The Path of the Just,* Feldheim Publ. Jerusalem and New York, 1974 (sec. edition) tr. by S. Silverstein.

doctrine" *(dhamma-hadaya)*. This great Heart is in fact the centre of all the bloodstreams pulsating through the entire body of the doctrine *(dhamma-kaya)*. . . .

This ancient Way of Mindfulness is as practicable today as it was 2,500 years ago. It is as applicable in the lands of the West as in the East; in the midst of life's turmoil as well as in the peace of the monk's cell. . . .

Right Mindfulness is, in fact, the indispensable basis of Right Living and Right Thinking—everywhere, at any time, for everyone. It has a vital message for all: not only for the confirmed follower of the Buddha and his Doctrine (Dhamma), but for all who endeavour to master the mind that is so hard to control, and who earnestly wish to develop its latent faculties of greater strength and greater happiness.[4]

Mindfulness is practiced not only in daily meditation exercises in which awareness of breathing is the central issue, but it is equally to be applied to every moment of daily living. It means not to do anything in a distracted manner, but in full concentration of what is at hand, whether this is walking, eating, thinking, seeing, so that living becomes fully transparent by full awareness. "Mindfulness comprises the entire man and his whole field of experience,"[5] says Nyanaponika. It extends to every sphere of being: to the *state* of one's mind and to the mental *contents* of one's mind. Every experience, if it is done with mindfulness, is clear, distinct, real, and hence not automatic, mechanical, diffuse. The person who has reached a state of full mindfulness is wide-awake, aware of reality in its depth and concreteness; he is concentrated and not distracted.

The first of the exercises that lead to an increase in mindfulness is *breathing*. It is, as the author emphasizes, "an exercise in *mindfulness*, and not a *breathing* exercise." And:

In the case of the Buddhist practice there is no "retention" of breath or any other interference with it. There is just a quiet "bare

4. *Heart of Buddhist Meditation*, pp. 7, 8.
5. Ibid., p. 57.

observation" of its natural flow, with a firm and steady, but easy and "buoyant" attention, i.e., without strain or rigidity. The length or shortness of breathing is noticed, but not deliberately regulated. By regular practice, however, a calming, equalizing and deepening of the breath will result quite naturally; and the tranquillization and deepening of the breath-rhythm will lead to a tranquillization and deepening of the entire life-rhythm. In this way, Mindfulness of Breathing is an important factor of physical and mental health, though that is only incidental to the practice.[6]

In classic Buddhist meditation as described by Nyanaponika, mindfulness of breathing is followed by that of bodily postures, by clear comprehension of all functions of the body; then by clear awareness of feeling, of one's state of mind (self-knowledge), and of mental contents.

It is impossible in this short survey to report with sufficient clarity and detail Buddhist meditation as practiced by the Theravada school, to which Nyanaponika Mahathera belongs. Hence, to anyone who is seriously interested in awareness-widening meditation, I can only recommend studying *The Heart of Buddhist Meditation*. There is one qualification, however, that I want to add to this suggestion, although the author himself has mentioned that this method "is not only for the confirmed followers of the Buddha": The author is a most learned Buddhist monk and he presents Buddhist doctrine in its traditional form. For many, like myself, who do not agree with a number of Buddhist doctrines such as reincarnation and a certain life-negating tendency in Hinayana Buddhism, or with techniques suggested to convince oneself of the futility of craving by imagining the foulness of the dead body it is difficult to practice meditation in exactly the way which the author describes. Nevertheless, it seems to me that even without the doctrines just mentioned, there are two core doctrines acceptable to many who, like myself, are not Buddhists, yet are deeply impressed by the core of Buddhist teaching. I refer first of all to the doctrine that the goal of

---

6. Ibid., p. 61.

life is to overcome greed, hate, and ignorance. In this respect Buddhism does not basically differ from Jewish and Christian ethical norms. More important, and different from the Jewish and Christian tradition, is another element of Buddhist thinking: the demand for optimal awareness of the processes inside and outside oneself. Buddhism having been a revolutionary movement against Hindu orthodoxy, and severely persecuted for its atheism for centuries, is characterized by a degree of rationality and critical thought not to be found in Western religions. The essence of its teaching is that—by a full awareness of reality—greed, hate, and hence suffering can be overcome. It is a philosophical-anthropological system that arrives at norms for living as a consequence of analyzing the observable data about man's existence.

Nyanaponika Mahathera himself has expressed his point with great clarity. He describes the function of mindfulness as "producing an increasingly greater clarity and intensity of consciousness and presenting a picture of actuality that is increasingly purged of any falsifications."[7] He speaks of meditation as leading to "a natural, close and more friendly contact" with "subconsciousness."[8] "In that way," he writes, "the subconsciousness will become more 'articulate' and more amenable to control, i.e., capable of being co-ordinated with, and helpful to, the governing tendencies of the conscious mind. By reducing the element of the unpredictable and of the unmanageable emerging from the subconscious, self-reliance will receive a safer basis."[9]

He ends the description of the practice of mindfulness by emphasizing one of the most significant elements in Buddhist thinking, its insistence on independence and freedom. He writes: "In its spirit of self-reliance, *Satipatthana* [mindfulness] does not require any elaborate *technique* or external devices. The daily life is its working material. It has nothing to do with any exotic cults

---

7. Ibid., p. 26.
8. Ibid., p. 82. The term "subconsciousness" has been chosen by the author for his own good reasons; I would prefer the term "unconscious," because it does not imply a spatial location below consciousness.
9. Ibid., p. 82.

or rites nor does it confer 'initiations' or 'esoteric knowledge' in any way other than by self-enlightenment."[10]

We have seen that the essence of Buddhist meditation is to achieve optimal awareness of reality, more particularly of one's body and of one's mind. Even for one who follows the method of Buddhist meditation in its traditional form, the question arises whether this form cannot be enlarged by adding new dimensions of awareness that in the traditional method are only hinted at. It seems to me that there are indeed two such extensions of Buddhist meditation, although they can be practiced fruitfully without any connection with Buddhist meditation, or in connection with other kinds of meditation, or simply with the practice of stillness.

As far as methods conducive to greater awareness of the body are concerned, they have already been mentioned above: I refer to "sensory awareness," "the art of moving," and the T'ai Chi Chuan.

The other aspect of Buddhist meditation is "greater clarity and intensity of consciousness and presenting a picture of actuality that is increasingly purged of any falsifications."[11] Nyanaponika Mahathera himself mentions "a more friendly contact with unconsciousness," and it is indeed going only one step further to suggest that the *psychoanalytic method,* whose aim is insight of the unconscious aspects of one's mind may be an important addition to Buddhist meditation. Nyanaponika, to whom I am deeply indebted for his profound and patient explanations of Buddhist meditation and Buddhist doctrine, agreed that such a psychoanalytic search may very well be considered an addition to traditional Buddhist meditation. But once more I want to emphasize that in my opinion the psychoanalytic method as a means to optimal awareness is a method in its own right and valid without any connection with Buddhist or any other method of meditation.

---

10. Ibid., p. 82.
11. Ibid., p. 26.

PART IV

11. Psychoanalysis and Self-Awareness

At this point we make connection again with the previous discussion on self-awareness, provided that it is true that psychoanalysis can also have a "trans-therapeutic" function and that it is one of the most adequate methods for increasing self-awareness, and hence inner liberation.

This assumption is not shared by everybody. Probably most laymen and professionals define the essence of psychoanalysis as a cure for neurosis achieved by bringing to our awareness repressed sexual memories and the affects connected with them. The concept of awareness in this definition is very restricted in comparison with the one presented earlier in the text; it refers essentially to awareness of repressed libidinal forces, and its aim is also restricted to the therapeutic one in the conventional sense, i.e., to help the patient to reduce his individual "extra-suffering" to the general, socially accepted level of suffering.

I believe that this restricted concept of psychoanalysis does not do justice to the real depth and scope of Freud's discoveries. Freud himself can be quoted as a witness for the justification of this statement. When in the twenties he changed his theory from the crucial role of the conflict between libido and ego to the crucial role of the conflict between two biologically rooted instincts, that of the life instinct and the death instinct, he had factually given up the libido theory, even though he tried to reconcile the old and the new theories.[1] Furthermore, when

---

1. The change from the older to the new theory and Freud's not very successful attempt to reconcile them are discussed in detail in the Appendix of E.

Freud defined what he considered to be the essence of psychoanalytic theory, he mentioned repression, resistance, and transference but not the libido theory and not even the "Oedipus
complex."

In order to appreciate the fact that what *seems* to be the nuclear
concept of psychoanalysis—the libido theory—may not in reality
be Freud's most important discovery and not even a correct one,
we must consider a more general phenomenon. Every creative
thinker can only think in terms of the thought patterns and cate-
gories of his culture. Often his most original thought is not
"thinkable" and hence he has to formulate his thought by dis-
torting (or narrowing down) his discoveries in order that they be
thinkable. The original idea must be expressed at first in erroneous
forms, until the development of thought, based on the development of society, permits that the older formulations can be liberated from their time-bound errors and assume a significance that
is even greater than the author himself may have believed.

Freud, deeply imbued with the philosophy of bourgeois materialism, found it unthinkable to assume that a psychic force
should motivate man, unless it was identifiable as being simultaneously a physiological force; sexual energy was the only force
that combined both qualities.

Freud's theory of the conflict between libido and ego as the
central conflict in man was therefore a necessary assumption,
which enabled him to express his fundamental discovery in
"thinkable" terms. Freed from the shackles of the libido theory,
the essence of psychoanalysis can be defined as the discovery of the
 significance of conflicting *tendencies in man,* of the power of the
"resistance" to fight against the awareness of these conflicts, of
the rationalizations that make it appear that there is no conflict,
and of the liberating effect of becoming aware of the conflict,
and of the pathogenic role of unsolved conflicts.

Freud not only discovered these general principles but was the
first to devise concrete methods of how to study the repressed:

Fromm, *The Anatomy of Human Destructiveness* (New York: Holt, Rinehart and
Winston, 1973).

In dreams, symptoms, and in behavior of daily life. The conflicts between sexual impulses and the ego and superego form only a small part of the conflicts that, in their tragic failure to be solved as well as in their productive solutions, are central in many people's existence.

Freud's historical significance does not lie in the discovery of the effects of repressing sexual striving. This was a bold thesis at his time, but if it had been Freud's greatest contribution he would never have had the jolting influence he had. This influence was due to the fact that he smashed the conventional view that man's thinking and his being are identical, that he unmasked hypocrisy; that his theory was a critical one, inasmuch as he questioned all conscious thought, intentions, and virtues and demonstrated how often they are nothing but forms of resistance to hide the inner reality.

If one interprets Freud's theories in the sense that I just outlined, then it is not difficult to proceed and to assume that the function of psychoanalysis transcends the narrower therapeutic one and that it can be a method for achieving inner liberation by awareness of repressed conflicts.

*   *   *

Before entering into a discussion of the trans-therapeutic function of psychoanalysis, I deem it necessary to express some warnings and to point to some dangers of psychoanalysis. In spite of the general rush to be psychoanalyzed when a person faces difficulties in living, there are a number of reasons why *not* to try psychoanalysis, at least not as a first-aid station.

The first reason is that it is an easy way out from the need to try to solve one's difficulty oneself. Together with the ideals of smoothness, painlessness, and effortlessness discussed earlier, there is also a widespread belief that life should not offer any conflicts, agonizing choices, painful decisions. Such situations are considered more or less abnormal or pathological and not a necessary part of ordinary living. Of course, machines have no conflicts; therefore, why should living automatons have any, unless there is a defect in their construction or their functioning?

What could be more naïve? Only the most superficial, alienated kind of living may not require conscious decisions, although
it does generate plenty of neurotic and psychosomatic symptoms
such as ulcers or hypertension as a manifestation of unconscious
conflicts. If a person has not entirely lost the capacity to *feel,* if
he has not become a robot, he can scarcely avoid facing painful
decisions.

This is the case, for instance, in the process of a son's liberation
from his parents, which can be very painful if he senses the hurt
he inflicts upon them by the separation. But he would be naïve
to believe that the fact that this decision is painful and difficult
is an indication that it is neurotic and hence that he needs to be
analyzed.

Another example is that of divorce. The decision to divorce
one's wife (or husband) is one of the most painful ones to make,
yet it can be necessary for the sake of ending continuous conflict
and severe hindrance of one's own development. In this situation
thousands of persons believe they must be analyzed because they
must have a "complex" that makes the decision so difficult. At
least, that is what they consciously think. In reality they often
have other motives; most frequently, all they want is to postpone
the decision, rationalizing that they must first find out, through
being analyzed, all their unconscious motivations. Many couples
agree that both go to an analyst before they make the decision.
That the analysis may last two, three, or four years does not
bother them particularly. On the contrary, the longer it lasts, the
longer are they protected from making the decision. But beyond
this procrastination of decision, with the help of analysis, many
of these people have other hopes, consciously or unconsciously.
Some hope that the analyst will eventually make the decision for
them, or advise them what to do directly or via "interpretation."
Even if this does not work they have a second expectation: that
psychoanalysis will result in such inner clarity that they will be
able to decide without difficulty and with no pain involved.
When both expectations fail to materialize, they may nevertheless
achieve a doubtful advantage: Either they are so tired of talking
about the divorce that they decide, without much further

thought, either to divorce or to stay together. In the latter case they have at least a topic to talk about that interests both of them: their own feelings, fears, dreams, etc. In other words, this analysis has given some substance to their communication, although mainly one of *talking about* feelings rather than feeling differently toward each other.

To the examples given so far many others could be added: a man deciding to give up a well-paid for a more interesting and less lucrative job, a government official's choice to resign or act against his conscience, a person participating in a political protest movement and risking losing his job or being blacklisted, a priest's decision to let his conscience speak the truth and risk being dismissed from his order and losing all material and psychic security that belonging to it gives.

It appears that people much more rarely go to a psychoanalyst for help in the conflict between the demands of conscience and those of self-interest than in connection with family and personal conflicts as described in the previous examples. One might suspect that these family and personal conflicts are put in the foreground in order to cover up the much more fundamental, severe, and painful conflicts between conscience, integrity, authenticity, and self-interest. Usually these latter conflicts are not even seen as such but are quickly shoved away as irrational, romantic, "infantile" impulses that need not and should not be pursued any further. Yet they are the crucial conflicts of everyone's life, much more crucial than divorce or not divorce—which, most of the time, is only the replacement of an older by a newer model.

Another reason for not trying psychoanalysis lies in the danger that one is seeking—and finds—in the psychoanalyst a new father figure on whom one becomes dependent, thus blocking one's own further development.

The classic psychoanalyst will say that the opposite is true, that the patient discovers the unconscious dependency on a father in the transference to the analyst, and by analyzing the transference dissolves the transference as well as the original attachment to a father. Theoretically this is true, and practically it sometimes happens. But many times something quite different occurs. The analysand may have indeed cut the tie with father, but under the disguise of this independence builds up a new tie, that to the analyst. He becomes the authority, the adviser, the wise teacher, the kind friend—the central figure in one's life. That this happens so often has, among others, one reason in a shortcoming of classic Freudian theory: Freud's basic assumption was that all "irrational" phenomena, such as the need for a strong authority, inordinate ambition, avarice, sadism, masochism were rooted in the conditions of early childhood; these conditions were the key to the understanding of later development (even though theoretically he recognized constitutional factors as having some influence). Thus, the need for a strong authority was explained as being rooted in the factual helplessness of the child; and when the same attachment appeared in relationship to the analyst, it was explained as "transference," i.e., as being transferred from one object (the father) to another (the analyst). Such transference occurs and is an important psychic phenomenon.

But this explanation is too narrow. Not only is the child powerless, the adult is powerless too. This powerlessness is rooted in the very conditions of man's existence, in the "human situation." Aware of the many dangers that threaten him, of death, of the insecurity of the future, of the limitations of his knowledge, man cannot help feeling powerless. This existential powerlessness of the individual has been greatly increased by his *historical* powerlessness, which existed in all societies in which an elite established its exploitation of the majority by making them much more powerless than they would be in a state of natural democracy as it existed in the most primitive forms of human societies,[2] or as it might in future forms based on solidarity rather than antagonism.

Thus, for both existential and historical reasons, man seeks to attach himself to "magic helpers," in many forms: shamans, priests, kings, political leaders, fathers, teachers, psychoanalysts, as well as to many institutions such as Church and State. Those who have exploited man usually offered themselves—and were

---

2. Cf. the discussion of this topic in my book *The Anatomy of Human Destructiveness*.

readily accepted—as such father figures. One preferred to obey men who, allegedly, meant well rather than to admit to oneself that one obeyed out of fear and impotence.

Freud's discovery of the phenomenon of transference had much wider implications than he himself, within the frame of reference of the thinking of his time, could see. In discovering transference he discovered a special case of *one* of the most powerful strivings in man, that of idolatry (alienation). It is striving that is rooted in the ambiguity of man's existence and that has the aim of finding an answer to the uncertainty of life by transforming a person, an institution, an idea into an absolute, i.e., into an idol by the submission to which the illusion of certainty is created. It is hardly possible to overestimate the psychological and social significance of idolatry in the course of history, that great illusion which hobbles activity and independence.

The clientele of psychoanalysts are, largely, liberal members of the middle and upper-middle classes, for whom religion has ceased to play an effective role, and who have no passionately held political convictions. For them no god, emperor, pope, rabbi, or charismatic political leader fills the void. The psychoanalyst becomes a mixture of guru, scientist, father, priest, or rabbi; he does not demand hard tasks, he is friendly, he dissolves all the real problems of life—social, economic, political, religious, moral, philosophical—into psychological ones. Thus he reduces them to the status of rationalizations of incestuous wishes, patricidal impulses, or anal fixation. The world becomes simple, accountable, manageable, and comfortable when it is reduced to this bourgeois mini-cosmos.

* * *

Another danger in conventional psychoanalysis lies in the fact that the patient often only pretends that he wants to change. If he suffers from bothersome symptoms, such as difficulties in sleeping, impotence, fear of authorities, being unhappy in relation to the opposite sex, or a general feeling of malaise, he of course wants to be rid of his symptoms. Who wouldn't? But he is unwilling to experience the pain and anguish that are inseparable from the process of growing and becoming independent. How does he solve the dilemma? He expects that if he only follows the "basic rule"—to say whatever comes to mind without censoring it—he will be cured without pain or even effort; to put it briefly, he believes in "salvation by talking." But there is no such thing. Without effort and willingness to experience pain and anxiety, nobody grows, in fact nobody achieves anything worth achieving.

One more danger of conventional analysis is something that one should expect least: The "cerebralization" of affective experience. Freud's intention was clearly the opposite: he wanted to break through conventional conscious thought processes and arrive at the experience, the raw, unrationalized, illogical feelings and visions behind the smooth surface of daylight thought. He indeed found it in the hypnotic state, in the dream, in the language of symptoms, and in many usually unobserved small details of behavior. But in the practice of psychoanalysis the original goal withered away and became an ideology. More and more, psychoanalysis became transformed into a kind of historical research into the development of an individual, heavily overloaded with theoretical explanation and constructions.

The analyst had a number of theoretical assumptions and he used the patient's associations as documentary proofs for the correctness of his theories. He was in good faith because he was convinced of the truth of the dogma, and he believed that the material the analysand offered must be profound and genuine precisely because it fitted the theory. The method became increasingly one of *explanation*. Here is a typical example: A patient suffers from obesity caused by compulsive eating habits. The analyst interprets her compulsion and the ensuing fatness as being rooted in her unconscious desire to swallow her father's semen and to be pregnant through him. The fact that she has no direct memories of ever having had such wishes and phantasies is explained by the repression of this painful infantile material; but, on the basis of the theory, this origin is "reconstructed" and the rest of the analysis consists largely in the analyst's attempt to use the patient's further associations and dreams in order to prove the correctness of the reconstruction. It is assumed that when the patient has fully "understood" the meaning of the symptom, she will be cured from it.

Basically, the method of this kind of interpretation is to cure by explanation; the crucial question is "*Why* has the neurotic symptom been formed?" While the patient is asked to go on associating, he is engaged intellectually in the research about the origin of his symptoms. What was meant to be an experiential method has become transformed—in fact, though not in theory—into an intellectual search. Even if the theoretical premises were correct, such a method could not lead to changes, except those that are brought about by any method of suggestion. If a person is analyzed for a considerable time and told that this or that factor is the cause of his neurosis, he will easily be ready to believe that this is so and relinquish his symptom on the basis of the faith that the discovery of the roots has brought about the cure. This mechanism is so frequent that no scientist would accept the cure of a symptom as being caused by a given medicine unless the patient is unaware whether he got the medicine or a placebo—and not only the patient, but the physician also, in order to make sure that he himself is not influenced by his own expectations ("double-blind test").

The danger of intellectualization is all the greater today, when the prevailing alienation from one's own affective experience leads to an almost total intellectual approach to oneself and the rest of the world.

*   *   *

In spite of the dangers inherent in the conventional practice of psychoanalysis, I must confess that after over forty years of psychoanalytic practice I am more convinced than ever that psychoanalysis properly understood and practiced has great potential as a means to help man. This holds true for the traditional realm of psychoanalysis, the cure of neuroses.

But we are not concerned here primarily with psychoanalysis as a therapy for neuroses but with a *new* function of analysis, which I call *transtherapeutic analysis*. It may begin as a therapeutic analysis but not stop when the symptoms are cured, and proceed to new goals that transcend therapy; or it may start out with a trans-therapeutic goal, where there are no significant psychopathological problems to be resolved. Decisive is that its goals go beyond restoring a patient to "normalcy." This aim was not in Freud's mind as far as he was a therapist, although it is not as foreign to him as one might assume. While his aim for therapy was that of adjustment to "normal" functioning ("to be able to work and to love"), his great ambition did not lie in the field of therapy but in the creation of an enlightenment movement, based on the last step enlightenment could make: the awareness and control of irrational passions. This ambition was so strong that Freud often acted as a political leader who had to conquer the world with his "movement," rather than as a scientist.[3]

The transtherapeutic goal is that of man's self-liberation by optimal self-awareness; of the attaining of well-being, independence; of the capacity to love; and of critical, dis-illusioned thinking, of being rather than having.

Trans-therapeutic ("humanistic") psychoanalysis revises some of Freud's theories, particularly the libido theory, as being too small a basis for the understanding of man. Instead of centering on sexuality and the family, it claims that the specific conditions of human existence and the structure of society are of more fundamental importance than the family, and that the passions motivating man are essentially not instinctive but a "second nature" of man, formed by the interaction of existential and social conditions.

In the past I sometimes used the term "humanistic" psychoanalysis and then dropped it, partly because it was taken over by a group of psychologists whose views I did not share, partly because I wanted to avoid the impression that I was establishing a new "school" of psychoanalysis. As far as schools of psychoanal-

---

3. Cf. E. Fromm, *Sigmund Freud's Mission* (New York: Harper & Bros., 1959); also Freud's letters to Jung, which are sometimes shocking by the predominance of political vs. scientific and human interests: *The Freud/Jung Letters,* ed. W. McGuire (Princeton: Princeton University Press, 1974).

ysis are concerned, experience has shown that they are detrimental to the theoretical development of psychoanalysis and to the competence of their practitioners. This is obvious in the case of Freud's school. Freud, I believe, was hindered in changing his theories because he had to hold together his adherents by a common ideology. If he had changed basic theoretical positions, he would have deprived his adherents of unifying dogmas. Furthermore, the "school" and its approbation had devastating effects on its members. Being properly "ordained" gave to many the necessary moral support to feel competent for their task without having to make further great efforts in learning. What holds true for the orthodox school holds true, from my observation, for all the rest. These observations have led me to the conviction that the formation of psychoanalytic schools is undesirable and only leads to dogmatism and incompetence.[4]

Also the technical procedure is different; more active, direct, and challenging. The basic aim, nevertheless, is that of classic psychoanalysis: the uncovering of unconscious strivings, the recognition of resistance, transference, rationalization, and the interpretation of dreams as the "royal road" to the understanding of the unconscious.

One qualification should be added to this description. A person who seeks optimal growth may also have neurotic symptoms and thus need analysis as a therapy. A person who has not been completely alienated, who has remained sensitive and able to feel, who has not lost the sense of dignity, who is not yet "for sale," who can still suffer over the suffering of others, who has not acquired fully the having mode of existence—briefly, a person who has remained a person and not become a thing—cannot help feeling lonely, powerless, isolated in present-day society. He cannot help doubting himself and his own convictions, if not his sanity. He cannot help suffering, even though he can experience moments of joy and clarity that are absent in the life of his

---

4. These theoretical views are dealt with in many of my writings; the most concise formulation is to be found in E. Fromm, *The Anatomy of Human Destructiveness*.

"normal" contemporaries. Not rarely will he suffer from a neurosis that results from the situation of a sane man living in an insane society, rather than that of the more conventional neurosis of a sick man trying to adapt himself to a sick society. In the process of going further in his analysis, i.e., of growing to greater independence and productivity, his neurotic symptoms will cure themselves. In the last analysis, all forms of neuroses are indications of the failure to solve the problem of living adequately.

12. Self-Analysis

If the exploration of one's unconscious should be a part of meditation, the question arises whether a person can analyze himself as part of his meditation practice. No doubt this is very difficult, and it is preferable that he be introduced into the practice of self-analyzing by analytic work with a competent analyst.

The first question to answer is what analyst is competent for this kind of transtherapeutic analysis. If the analyst himself has not had this goal, he would scarcely understand what the patient wants and needs. Not that he must have achieved this goal by himself, but that he is on the way toward it. Since the number of analysts pursuing this goal is relatively small, it is not easy to find such an analyst. One rule should be observed here—as in choosing an analyst for strictly therapeutic reasons—that one should thoroughly investigate the psychoanalyst through people who know him well (patients and colleagues) and not believe in big names or impressive offices as recommendations; one should also be skeptical of enthusiastic reports by patients who have idolized their analyst; one should try to form an impression of the analyst in one or two, or even ten first interviews and watch him as carefully as he is supposed to watch you. To work for years with a "wrong" analyst can be as harmful as being married for years to the wrong person.

As for the "school" an analyst comes from, that in itself says little. The "existentialist" psychoanalysts are supposed to be more concerned with problems of human goals—and some are. Others understand little, and simply use a philosophical jargon taken from Husserl, Heidegger, or Sartre as a gimmick, without really penetrating the depth of the patient's personality. Jungians have the reputation of being those most concerned with the spiritual and religious needs of the patient. Some of them are, but many, in their enthusiasm for myths and analogies, fail to penetrate into the depths of the patient's individual life and into his *personal* unconscious.

The "Neo-Freudians" are not necessarily more reliable than the others. *Not* to be a Freudian—is not enough! Some indeed approach analysis from a standpoint that is related to the one outlined here; many others have a rather superficial approach, which lacks depth and critical thought. Perhaps the school furthest away from the one I suggest are the orthodox Freudians, because the libido theory and the one-sided emphasis on childhood experience stand in their way. Yet, in spite of that doctrine, there are probably a few whose personal qualities and philosophy make them acceptable guides to the full awareness of one's inner reality. In sum, I believe the competence of an analyst is less a matter of the school to which he belongs than of his personality, his character, his capacity for critical thinking, and his personal philosophy.

Closely related to the person of the analyst is the *method* he uses. First of all, I do not believe that an analysis aimed at teaching self-analysis need last very long. In general, two hours a week for six months should suffice. This requires a special technique: The analyst should not be passive; after listening to the patient for 5 to 10 hours he should have an idea of the patient's unconscious structure and of the intensity of his resistance. The analyst then should be able to confront the patient with his findings, analyze his reactions and, particularly, his resistance. Furthermore, he should analyze from the beginning the patient's dreams, using them for guidance of his own diagnosis, and then communicate their interpretation (as well as that of the rest) to the patient.

At the end of this period, the patient should have become sufficiently acquainted with his own unconscious and lowered his resistance to the point where he can continue the analysis on his own, beginning his daily self-analysis for the rest of his life. I say this because there is no limit to the knowledge of oneself, and I can say from my own experience with daily self-analysis over the last forty years that at no time until now has it happened that I did not discover something new or deepen already-known material. However, it may be useful, especially in the beginning of self-analysis, to return to work with the analyst, if one finds oneself "stymied." But this should be done only as a last resort, otherwise it is too tempting to renew the attachment.

An introductory analysis as preparation for self-analysis is the most desirable procedure. This procedure is very difficult not only because there are not many psychoanalysts whose own personality capacitates for this work, but also because the routine of their practice is not geared to seeing patients for six months and then to seeing them again only occasionally, if at all. This type of work requires not only a special kind of interest but also a rather flexible schedule. I believe that if transtherapeutic self-analysis became more widespread, a number of psychoanalysts would specialize in this kind of work, or at least devote half of their working time to it.

But what if one does not find the proper analyst or for any number of reasons cannot go to the place where he practices or cannot afford it financially? Is self-analysis, in such a case, possible?

The answer to this question depends on a number of factors. First of all it depends on the intensity of the will to achieve the goal of liberation. And even this will, as such, cannot become effective except for the fact that the human brain has a built-in tendency for health and well-being—i.e., for the attainment of all those conditions that further the growth and development of the individual and the human species.[1] That this health-preserving tendency exists in the somatic sector of living is well known—and all that medicine can do is remove the obstacles to the efficacy of these tendencies and support them. Indeed, most

---

1. For this assumption, cf. my discussion in *The Anatomy of Human Destructiveness*.

illnesses cure themselves without any kind of intervention. That the same holds true for mental well-being is beginning to be seen again, recently, although it was well known to an older, less technical-interventionist age.

Unfavorable factors for self-analysis are states of serious pathology, which are even difficult enough to deal with in a prolonged "regular" analysis. In addition, an extremely important factor lies in certain circumstances of a person's life: If, for example, a person does not have to earn a living because he lives from inherited money or from the money of his parents (or of his wife or husband), he has a worse chance than one who is forced to work and hence can less well afford to insulate himself. Someone who lives in a group in which everybody suffers the same defect will be prone to accept his group's values as normal. Another negative condition is a case in which a person makes a living in such a manner that his neurotic qualities are an asset and where an inner change might endanger his livelihood; we think, here, of an entertainer or actor whose narcissism is a necessary condition for his success, or of a bureaucrat who might lose his job if he lost his submissiveness. Finally, the cultural and spiritual condition of a person is of great significance. Whether some contact with philosophical, religious, or critical political thought exists or whether he has never looked beyond the culturally patterned views of his environment and social class, makes a great deal of difference, often a decisive one. And, finally, mere intelligence as such does not appear to be a decisive factor. Sometimes intellectual brilliance only serves the purposes of resistance.

13. Methods of Self-Analysis

It would require a book in itself to write in full about how to learn to analyze oneself. Hence I must restrain myself here to a few simple suggestions.

Before one can even begin, one must have learned to be still, to sit relaxed, and to concentrate. When these first conditions are achieved—at least to some degree—one can proceed in different ways that by no means exclude each other.

(1) One may try to remember the thoughts that were intruding while one tried to be still, and then "feel one's way into them" with the aim of seeing whether they have any connection, and what it might be. Or one may proceed by observing certain symptoms such as feeling tired (in spite of sufficient sleep), or depressed, or angry, and then "feel around" what it was a reaction to and what was the unconscious experience behind the manifest feeling.

I intentionally do not say "to think," because one does not arrive at an answer by theoretical thought; at best, one arrives at a theoretical speculation. What I mean by "feeling around" is an imaginative "tasting" of various possible feelings until, if one has succeeded, a certain realization appears with clarity as being the root of the conscious experience of, say, tiredness. An example: One tries to imagine previous instances of such tiredness and whether, later on, one became aware of the cause. One imagines several possibilities that could be at the bottom of the tiredness, such as a difficult task one tried to postpone instead of facing the difficulty, an ambivalent feeling toward a friend or a loved person, a criticism that might have hurt one's narcissism to the extent of causing a slight depression, a meeting with a person in which one pretended a friendliness that was not genuine.

A more complex example is the following: A man has fallen in love with a girl. Suddenly, after some months, he feels tired, depressed, listless. He might try to find all sorts of rationalizing explanations, such as that his work is not going well (which may indeed be caused by the same factor that causes the tiredness) or that he is disappointed and saddened by political developments. Or he may acquire a severe cold and thus find a satisfactory answer. But if he is sensitive toward his own feelings, he may observe that recently he has tended to find fault in little things with the girlfriend, that he had a dream in which she had an ugly face and cheated on him. Or he may notice that while he was always very eager to see her, he has now found reasons that make it necessary to postpone planned visits. These and many other little signs may indicate to him that something is wrong in his relationship with her. If he concentrates on this feeling, it suddenly may dawn on him that his picture of her has changed, that in the first blossoming of his erotic and sexual attraction to her he had not noticed certain negative traits and that her sweet smile seems now to be calculated and actually cold.

He may trace back this change in his judgment to a certain evening when he had entered a room and watched her talking to other people, *before* she had seen him. At that moment he felt almost sick, but put away this feeling as "neurotic" or irrational— but then the next morning he had awakened with the depressed feeling from which he has suffered, by now, for several weeks. He had tried to repress the new awareness, and his doubts, because on the stage of conscious life the script of love and admiration was still being acted out. The conflict showed only in the indirect form of being stymied, of being listless and depressed because he could neither pursue his "love affair" with a joyful and honest heart nor break it off, because he had repressed the awareness of the change in his feelings. Once his eyes are open, he may regain his sense of reality, see clearly what he feels, and with real pain—but without depression—end the relationship.

Here is another example of the analysis of a symptom: A bachelor in his forties suffers from the obsessional fear, whenever he has left his house, that he may not have turned off the electric stove, and that a fire will start and destroy the whole house, especially his valuable library. Consequently, he feels compelled to return to his house whenever he has left it—a compulsion that obviously disrupts his normal activities.

The symptom has a simple explanation. Almost five years ago, he had been operated on for cancer; his physician had dropped the remark that everything was fine, except for the possibility in the next five years of the spread of the malignant cells—"which can spread like a fire." The man was so frightened of this possibility that he repressed the thought totally from his awareness and substituted for it the fear that fire might spread in his house. While uncomfortable, this fear was much less tormenting than that of the return of cancer. When the repressed content of the fear became conscious, the fire-obsession disappeared without reviving the fear of cancer, helped largely by the circumstance that by then almost five years had passed since the operation, and the danger of further complications was largely reduced.

This process of "concientizacion" usually carries with it a feeling of relief, and even joy, even though the content itself may be nothing to be pleased about. In addition, whatever the newly discovered element is, following it up by "feeling around" further will quite likely lead to some new discoveries, or ramifications, the same day or later on. What is essential is not to fall into the trap of stating complex theoretical speculations.

(2) Another approach is one that corresponds to the method of free association. One lets go of one's thought control, permits one's thoughts to come in, and tries to scrutinize them with the aim of discovering hidden connections between them, points of resistance where one feels like stopping the train of thought—until certain elements come to the fore that heretofore had not been in one's awareness.

(3) Still another approach is an autobiographical one. By this I mean speculations about one's history, beginning with one's early childhood and ending with one's projected future development. Try to get a picture of significant events, of your early fears, hopes, disappointments, events that decreased your trust and faith in people, and in yourself.

Ask: On whom am I dependent? What are my main fears? Who was I meant to be at birth? What were my goals and how did they change? What were the forks of the road where I took the wrong direction and went the wrong way? What efforts did I make to correct the error and return to the right way? Who am I now, and who would I be if I had always made the right decisions and avoided crucial errors? Whom did I want to be long ago, now, and in the future? What is my image of myself? What is the image I wish others to have of me? Where are the discrepancies between the two images, both between themselves and with what I sense is my real self? Who will I be if I continue to live as I am living now? What are the conditions responsible for the development as it happened? What are the alternatives for further development open to me now? What must I do to realize the possibility I choose?

This autobiographical research should not consist of abstract constructions in terms of psychoanalytic theorizing, but should remain on the empirical level of "seeing," sensing, imagining, with theoretical thoughts reduced to a minimum.

(4) Closely related to the autobiographical approach is one that tries to uncover the discrepancies that exist between our conscious goals in life and those of which we are not aware, yet which determine our life. In many persons there are two such plots: A conscious, "official" one, as it were, which is the cover story for the secret plot that dominates our behavior. The discrepancy between the secret and the conscious plots is shown in many of the ancient Greek dramas, in which the "secret plot" is attributed to "fate" *(moira)*. *Moira* is the alienated form of man's unconscious plot, which is within him and which determines his life. The Oedipus drama for instance, shows this discrepancy with all clarity: Oedipus' secret plot is to kill his father and marry his mother; his conscious and intended life plot is to avoid this crime under all circumstances. Yet the secret plot is stronger; against his intention and without awareness of what he is doing, he lives according to the secret plot.

The degree of discrepancy between the conscious and unconscious plots varies enormously in many people. On the one end of the continuum are those persons for whom there is no secret plot because the person has grown so far that he has become entirely one with himself, and need not repress anything. On the other extreme there may be no secret plot because the person has identified with his "evil" self to a degree that he does not even try to pretend that there is a "better self." The former are sometimes called the "just ones," the "awakened ones"; the latter are severely sick people for whom a number of diagnostic labels could be used—but without adding to their understanding. The vast majority of men can be plotted on a continuum between the two extremes, yet even in this middle group an important distinction can be made: There are those whose conscious plot is an idealization of what they are actually striving for, so that the two plots are essentially similar. With others, the cover story is exactly the opposite of the secret plot; it serves only to hide it in order to follow it all the better.

It is in the cases of significant contradictions between the two plots that severe conflicts, insecurity, doubts, and waste of energy occur and, as a result, a number of manifest symptoms develop. How could it be otherwise when a person has constantly to use a great deal of energy in order to avoid being aware of the inner contradiction, to cease being plagued by deep doubts about his identity, and to repress his own dim sense of lack of genuineness and integrity. His only alternative is either to continue his state of malaise or to penetrate to the deeply repressed layers of experience, and the latter process is necessarily conducive to a good deal of anxiety.

Here are a few examples of secret plots: I remember a man—whom I knew well but did not analyze—who once told me the following dream:

"I sat at a coffin which served as a table. A meal was served on it, which I ate. Next, I was shown a book in which many great men had signed their names; I saw the names of Moses, Aristotle, Plato, Kant, Spinoza, Marx, and Freud. I was asked to sign my name as the last one; the book then was presumably to be closed forever."

The dreamer was a man with extraordinary ambition; despite great knowledge and brilliance, he had the greatest difficulty to write a book by himself and with ideas he had not taken from somebody else. He had a sadistic character, which was covered up by altruistic, radical ideas and occasional gestures of helpfulness to others. In the first part of his dream we see a thinly veiled necrophagous desire—the lunch served on the coffin expresses, if translated into noncensored clear text, the desire to eat the body in the coffin. (This is one of the frequent manifestations of what Freud called the "dream work," which translates the unacceptable latent dream thought into a harmless-sounding "manifest" dream text.) The second part of the dream is hardly censored at all. The dreamer's ambition is to have the fame of one of the greatest thinkers of the world; his selfishness is expressed in the fact that he wishes that with him the history of philosophy should be ended; no more great men should arise from which future generations could benefit. This secret pot of eating the corpses of great men—i.e., feeding himself on the masters of the past and becoming by this introjection a master himself—was unknown to this person and hidden from those around him, most of whom admired him for his brilliance, kindness, and benevolent ideas.

The outline of another secret plot: To save his mother from his cruel father, and through her admiration to become the greatest man in the world. Or another: To destroy every living soul in order to be left alone, thus being rid of his feeling of weakness and of fear of others. And another: To attach oneself to someone rich and powerful; to find his favor and to wait for his death in order to inherit everything he owns—material goods, ideas, and prestige. Still another: To experience the world as a prison made of food, the aim of life being to eat up the walls of his prison; eating becomes the goal of life; eating means liberation.

One could add many more plots, but not an unlimited number. Since the secret plots are all answers to the basic needs rooted in human existence, there are only a limited number because the number of man's existential needs is limited.

Does this mean that we are in reality traitors, liars, sadists, etc., and only cover this up and do not act it out in overt behavior? Indeed it *can* mean that, if to betray, to lie, to torture are dominant passions within ourselves, and with not merely a few this is precisely the case: These very persons will have the least impulse to make such discoveries.

With many others, however, these repressed trends are not dominant; when they become conscious, they come in conflict with the opposite passions and have a good chance of being defeated in the ensuing struggle. *Awareness* is a *condition* that makes this conflict more acute, but it does not "dissolve" the formerly repressed strivings simply by our act of becoming conscious of them.

(5) A fifth approach is to let one's thoughts and feelings be

centered around the goals of living, such as overcoming greed, hate, illusions, fears, possessiveness, narcissism, destructiveness, sadism, masochism, dishonesty, lack of authenticity, alienation, indifference, necrophilia, male patriarchal dominance or corresponding female submission, and to achieve independence, the capacity for critical thought, for giving, for loving. This approach consists in the attempt to uncover the unconscious presence of any of these "bad" traits, the way they are rationalized, how they form part of one's whole character structure, the conditions of their development. The process is often very painful and may arouse a great deal of anxiety. It requires that we become aware of being dependent, when we believe that we love and are loyal; that we become aware of our vanity (narcissism), when we believe ourselves to be nothing but kind and helpful; that we become aware of our sadism, when we believe that we want to do for others only what is good for them; that we discover our destructiveness, when we believe that it is our sense of justice that demands punishment; that we become aware of our cowardice, when we believe ourselves to be only prudent and "realistic"; that we become aware of our arrogance, when we believe that we behave with extraordinary humility; that we are aware that we are afraid of freedom, when we think that we are only motivated by the wish not to hurt anybody; that we become aware that we are insincere, when we only thought that we did not want to be rude; that we discover that we are treacherous, when we believe that we are being particularly objective. In short, as Goethe put it, only if we can "imagine ourselves as the author of any conceivable crime," and mean it, can we be reasonably sure of having dropped the mask and of being on the way to becoming aware of who we are.

At the moment when one discovers the narcissistic components of one's friendliness or the sadistic elements of one's helpfulness, the shock may be so intense that for a moment or a day one feels oneself to be an utterly worthless creature, of whom nothing good could be said. But if one does not permit oneself to be stopped by this shock and goes on analyzing, one may discover that the shock is so intense—because of the narcissistic expectations of oneself—that it will serve as a resistance to further analysis and that the negative strivings one has discovered are, after all, not the only driving forces within oneself. In those instances in which this is true, a person will likely follow his resistance and stop analyzing.

*   *   *

Since, as I pointed out in the earlier discussion of awareness, the capacity to see is not divisible, self-analysis must also be concerned with becoming aware of the reality in other persons as well as in social and political life. In fact, knowledge of others often precedes self-knowledge. The child at an early age observes adults, already dimly sensing the reality behind the façade, and he becomes aware of the person behind the persona. As adults we often observe unconscious strivings in others before we learn to observe them in ourselves. We must be aware of these hidden sectors in others, because what goes on in ourselves is not only *intrapsychic*, and thus to be understood by studying only what goes on within the four walls of our person, but it is *interpersonal;* that is to say, it is a net of relations between myself and others; I can see ourselves fully only inasmuch as I see myself in my relations to others, and in theirs to me.

To see himself without illusions would not be so difficult for the individual, were he not constantly exposed to being brainwashed and deprived of the faculty of critical thinking. He is made to think and feel things that *he* would not feel or think, were it not for uninterrupted suggestions and elaborate methods of conditioning. Unless he can see the real meaning behind the double-talk, the reality behind the illusions, he is unable to be aware of himself as he is, and is aware only of himself as he is supposed to be.

What can I know of myself as long as I do not know that the self I do know is largely a synthetic product; that most people—including myself—lie without knowing it, that "defense" means "war" and "duty" submission; that "virtue" means "obedience" and "sin" disobedience; that the idea that parents instinctively love their children is a myth; that fame is only rarely based on admirable human qualities, and even not too often on real achievements; that history is a distorted record because it is written by the victors; that over-modesty is not necessarily the proof of a lack of vanity; that loving is the opposite of craving and greed; that everyone tries to rationalize evil intentions and actions and to make them appear noble and beneficial ones; that the pursuit of power means the persecution of truth, justice and love; that present-day industrial society is centered around the principle of selfishness, having and consuming, and not on principles of love and respect for life, as it preaches. Unless I am able to analyze the unconscious aspects of the society in which I live, I cannot know who *I* am, because I don't know which part of me is *not* me.

*   *   *

In the following paragraphs I want to make some general remarks about the method of self-analysis.

It is crucially important that it be done, like meditation and concentration, regularly and "not if one is in the mood." If somebody says he has no time for it, he is simply saying that he does not consider it important. If he has no time, he can make time, and this is so obviously a matter of the importance he gives to self-analysis that it is useless to explain how he can make the time. I should like to add that I do not mean to imply that self-analysis become a ritual that does not permit any exception. There are, of course, occasions when it is practically impossible to do it, and that should be taken in one's stride. Altogether the process of self-analysis should not have the character of forced labor, done in a grim mood of duty, yet necessary in order to reach a certain goal. Quite aside from the result, the process in itself should be liberating and hence joyful, even though suffering, pain, anxiety, and disappointment are mixed in with it.

For anyone who cannot empathize with the passion to climb a mountain, it must appear that the ascent is mere drudgery and discomfort; and some think (I have heard this also in psychoanalytic interpretation of mountain climbing) that only a masochist could voluntarily choose to undergo such unpleasantness. The mountain climber will not deny the effort and the strain, yet this is part of his joy, and by no means would he want to miss it. "Effort" does not equal "effort"; "pain" does not equal "pain." The pains of labor are different from the pains of an illness. What matters is the entire context in which the effort is made or the pain is suffered, and which gives it its specific quality. This is a point somewhat difficult to grasp, because in our Western tradition duty and virtue are considered harsh taskmasters; in fact the best proof that one acts rightly is that it is unpleasant, the proof of the opposite that one likes to do it. The Eastern tradition is entirely different, and far superior in this respect. It bypasses the polarity between rigid, stiff discipline and lazy, slouching "comfort." It aims at a state of harmony, which is at the same time structuralized, "disciplined" (in the autonomous sense), alive, flexible, and joyful.

In self-analysis as well as in analysis *à deux* there is one difficulty of which we must be aware from the very beginning: that of the effects of verbalization.

Assuming I wake up in the morning and see a blue sky and a shining sun, I am fully aware of the scenery, it makes me happy and more alive, but the experience is an awareness of the sky, of my response to it, and no words come to mind such as: "This is a beautiful sunny day." Once those words form, and I begin to *think* about the scenery in these words, the experience has somewhat lost in intensity. When, instead, a melody comes to my mind that expresses joy, or a painting that expresses the same mood, nothing of the experience is lost.

The boundary between awareness of feeling and expression of feeling in words is very fluid. There is the completely non-verbalized experience, and close to it the experience in which a word appears like a vessel that "contains" the feeling and yet does not contain it; for the feeling is constantly flowing and it overflows the vessel. The word-vessel is more like a note in a musical score, which is a symbol for a tone but not the tone itself. The feeling may be still more closely related to the word, but as long as the word is still a "living word," it has done little harm to the feeling. But there comes a point where the word becomes separated from the feeling, i.e., also from the speaking person, and at this point the word has lost its reality, except as a combination of sounds.

Many people experience this change. They were aware of a strong, beautiful—or frightening—experience. A day later, when they want to remember it by putting it into words, they say a sentence that accurately describes the feeling, yet the sentence sounds foreign to them; it is felt as if it were entirely in their head, that it has no connection with what they felt when it happened.[1] When this happens, one should realize that something went wrong, and that one has begun juggling words, rather than become aware of inner reality; and one should begin to analyze the resistance that eggs one on to cerebralize feelings. Such thoughts about feelings should be treated like any other interfering thoughts.

Self-analysis should be done for at least 30 minutes every morning, if possible at the same time and place, and outside interference should be avoided as far as possible. It can be done also in walking, although in the streets of a big city there is too much unrest. But self-analysis, and particularly breathing and awareness "exercises," can be done whenever one is not occupied with something else. There are many occasions when one has to wait, or has "nothing to do," as in a subway or a plane. All these occasions should be used for one or another form of mindfulness rather than for starting to read a magazine, talking to somebody, or daydreaming. Once one has acquired the the habit of doing so, such situations when one has "nothing to do" become very welcome because they are enriching and enjoyable.

It is surprising that self-analysis has hardly been discussed in psychoanalytic literature; one might have expected that Freud's self-analysis, about which he himself reports in his dream interpretation, would have suggested to others to experiment in the

---

1. The process corresponds to one that is described in Hegelian and Marxian terminology as one of "exteriorization" *(Entäusserung)*, as long as the word is still connected with the feeling, leading to alienation *(Entfremdung)*, when the word has become independent from the feeling.

same direction. Maybe the fact that this has not been so can be explained by the assumption that the image of Freud became so idolized that it was quite natural that he could not have been analyzed by anyone else, but had to owe his "enlightenment," as it were, only to himself; that it is different with ordinary men. They could not be without a "creator," and Freud himself or the priests acting in his name had to enlighten them. Whatever the reasons may be for this lack of following up Freud's example, it was only, as far as I am aware, Karen Horney[2] who suggested self-analysis as a real possibility. In the case she describes, she deals mainly with an acute neurotic problem and its solution. The main point in this context is her warm recommendation of self-analysis, although she clearly saw the difficulties.

The main reason for the fact that self-analysis has been so neglected as a curative possibility lies probably in the conventional bureaucratic concepts of most analysts about their role and that of the "patient." As in general medicine, the sick person is transformed into a "patient" and the belief is fostered that he needs a professional to get cured.[3] He is not supposed to cure himself, since that would indeed break down the sacred bureaucratic difference between the professional healer and the nonprofessional sufferer. This bureaucratic attitude does much harm, too, in the process of "regular analysis," where the analyst if he wants sincerely to understand the "patient," must become himself a patient, his own, and forget that he is supposed to be the only "healthy," "normal," "rational" one of the two.

Perhaps the most important reason for the unpopularity of self-analysis is the idea that it is very difficult. In an analysis *à deux,* the analyst can call the other's attention to his rationalizations, resistances, and narcissism. In self-analysis one is in danger of going in circles and giving in to one's resistances and rationalizations without being aware that this is what one is doing. Indeed, it cannot be denied that self-analysis is difficult—but so is

2. K. Horney, *Self-Analysis* (New York: W. W. Norton, 1942).

3. Cf. Ivan Illich's critique of this situation in *Medical Nemesis: The Expropriation of Health* (New York: Pantheon, 1976).

every other path to well-being. No one has formulated this difficulty more succinctly than Spinoza, at the end of his *Ethics:*
(Book 5, prop. 42): "If the way which, as I have shown, leads
hither seems very difficult, it can nevertheless be found. It must
indeed be difficult since it is so seldom discovered, for if salvation
lay ready to hand and could be discovered without great labour,
how could it be possible that it should be neglected by almost
everybody? But all noble things are as difficult as they are rare."[4]

The difficulty might be discouraging if the question were to
reach or not to reach the final goal. But if, as we said before,
one is not craving for perfection, if one is not concerned with
the point of the way at which one arrives, but with the act of
walking in the right direction, the difficulties do not appear so
formidable. Most of all, self-analysis will result in such an increase
in inner clarity and well-being that one would not want to miss
it, in spite of all the difficulties.

*   *   *

Having recommended self-analysis as a fruitful method in the
search for self-liberation, I want to add that this recommendation
does not imply that it is a necessary step that everybody should
take. It is one which appeals to me and which I have recommended to others who use it with profit. There are many others
who will use other methods of concentration, stillness, and
awareness that are quite as useful. A very telling example was
Pablo Casals, who began every day by playing one of Bach's
unaccompanied cello concertos. Who could doubt that this was
the optimal method of self-liberation for him?

Yet even as far as the method of self-analysis is concerned, a
misunderstanding, I fear, could have crept between the reader
and myself. The process that I have described could be misunderstood as a daily moralistic search of conscience, which should be
the basis for a steady moral progression and a virtuous life. If the
reader's criticism were that I am opposed to ethical relativism, to

---

4. Quoted by E. Fromm, in *Man for Himself: An Inquiry into the Psychology
of Ethics* (New York: Rinehart and Co., 1947).

the arbitrariness of freedom, to the supreme value of everybody's "doing his own thing," regardless of what it is worth, I must plead guilty. But I refuse such a plea if the accusation were that I am anxiously concerned about man's straight pursuit of virtue and the horror of sin, and that I do not appreciate the fact that sin itself is often the very basis of progress.

In order to clarify this point, it must be kept in mind that the fundamental position from which self-analysis was discussed is the conception of living as a process and not as a sequence of fixed stages. In sinning, the seed for an upward movement is attained, in virtue the seed of decay may be contained. As a mystical principle says, "The descent is for the sake of the ascent"; sinning is not harmful but only stagnating and resting on what one has achieved.

There is still another possible misunderstanding I want to correct. It might sound as if self-analysis increases the tendency for being occupied with oneself; i.e., that it is the very opposite to the aim of getting rid of one's ego-boundness. Indeed, that can be an outcome, but only of an unsuccessful analysis. Self-analysis becomes a kind of cleansing ritual, not because one is so concerned with one's ego but because one wants to free oneself from egosim by analyzing its roots. Self-analysis becomes a daily practice that permits one to be minimally concerned with oneself the rest of the day. Finally, it becomes unnecessary, because there are no more obstacles to full being. I cannot write about this state, because I have not attained it.

At the end of this discussion of psychoanalysis, I believe one further qualification is necessary, which holds true for all psychological knowledge. If one starts out with the psychological understanding of one person, one is concerned with his *suchness*, his full individuality. Unless one has a picture of his individuality in all its details, one cannot begin to understand this particular person. If one's interest in a person shifts from the more superficial to the deeper levels, it shifts necessarily from the particular to the universal. This "universal" is not an abstraction, not a limited universal like the instinctive nature of man. It is the very essence of human existence, the "human condition," the needs that follow from it, the various answers to these needs. It is the content of the unconscious, which is common to all men because of the identity of the existential condition of all men and not because of some racial heritage, as Jung believed. One then experiences oneself and one's fellow man as variations of the theme "man," and maybe man as a variation of the theme of life. What matters is that which all men share, not that in which they differ. In the process of the full penetration of one's unconscious one discovers that we differ considerably in the quantitative aspects but are the same in the quality of our strivings. The exploration of the unconscious in depth is a way of discovering humanity in oneself and in every other human being; this discovery is not one of theoretical thought but of affective experience.

However, stressing the One in man must not in an undialectical fashion lead to the denial of the fact that man is also an individual; that, in fact, each person is a unique individual not identical with anyone ever to be born (perhaps with the exception of identical twins). Only paradoxical thinking, so much a part of Eastern logic, permits expression of the full reality: Man is a unique individual—man's individuality is sham and unreal. Man is "this and that" and man is "neither this nor that." The paradoxical fact is that the deeper I experience my own or another's unique individuality, the clearer I see through myself and him the reality of universal man, freed from all individual qualities, "the Zen Buddhists' man without rank and without title."

These considerations lead to the problem of the value and the dangers of individualism and, related to it, the psychological study of the individual. It is very apparent that, at present, individuality and individualism are highly esteemed and widely praised as values and as personal and cultural goals. But the value of individuality is very ambiguous. On the one hand, it contains the element of liberation from authoritarian structures that prevent the autonomous development of a person. If self-knowledge serves to become aware of one's *true* self, and to develop it rather than to introject a "foreign" self, imposed by the authorities, it is of great human value. In fact, the positive aspect of self-knowledge and psychology are so widely emphasized that it is scarcely necessary to add more words to this praise.

But it is extremely necessary to say something about the negative side of the cult of individuality, and its relation to psychology. One reason for this cult is obvious: The more individuality disappears in fact, the more it is exalted in words. Industry, television, habits of consumption pay homage to the individuality of the persons they manipulate: There is the name of the bank teller in his window and the initials on the handbag. In addition, the individuality of commodities is stressed: The alleged differences between cars, cigarettes, toothpaste, which are essentially the same (in the same price class), serve the purpose of creating the illusion of the individual man or woman freely choosing individual things. There is little awareness that the individuality is, at best, one of insignificant differences, for in all their essential features commodities and human beings have lost all individuality.

The apparent individuality is cherished as a precious possession. Even if people don't own capital, they own their individuality. Although they *are* not individuals, they *have* much individuality, and they are eager and proud to cultivate it. Since this individuality is one of small differences, they give the small, trivial differences the aspect of important, meaningful features.

Contemporary psychology has promoted and satisfied this interest in "individuality." People think about their "problems," talk about all the little details of their childhood history, but often what they say is glorified gossip about themselves and others, using psychological terms and concepts instead of the less sophisticated old-fashioned gossip.

Supporting this illusion of *individuality through trivial differences,* contemporary psychology has a still more important function; by teaching how people ought to react under the influence of different stimuli, psychologists become an important instrument for the manipulation of others and of oneself. Behaviorism has created a whole science that teaches the art of manipulation. Many business firms make it a condition for employment that their prospective employees submit to personality tests. Many books teach the individual how to behave, in order to impress people of the value of their own personality package or of the value of the commodity they sell. By being useful in all these respects, one branch of contemporary psychology has become an important part of modern society.

While this type of psychology is useful economically and as an illusion-producing ideology, it is harmful to human beings because it tends to increase their alienation. It is fraudulent when it pretends to be based on the ideas of "self-knowledge" as the humanistic tradition, up to Freud, had conceived it.

The opposite to adjustment psychology is radical, because it goes to the roots; it is critical, because it knows that conscious thought is mostly a fabric of illusions and falsehood. It is "salvific," because it hopes that the true knowledge of oneself and others liberates man and its conducive to his well-being. For anyone interested in psychological exploration it is necessary to be intensely aware of the fact that these two kinds of psychology have little more in common than the name, and that they follow contrary goals.

PART V

14. On the Culture of Having

Living has two dimensions. Man acts, does, produces, creates; in brief, he is active. But man is not acting in a void, not without body and not in an immaterial world: He has to deal with *things*. His acting refers to *objects*, animate or inanimate, which he transforms or creates.

The first "thing" he has to deal with is his own body; later, he has to deal with other things: With wood for fire or for shelter; with fruits, animals, and grain for food; with cotton and wool for clothing. As civilization develops, the realm of things man has to deal with enlarges many times. Weapons, houses, books, machines, ships, cars, planes come into existence and he has to deal with them all.

How does man deal with them? He produces them, he changes them, uses them to make other things, consumes them. Things themselves do nothing, except when man has constructed them in such a way that they do produce things by themselves.

With every culture the proportion between *things* and *acts* is different. In contrast to the great multitude of things modern man is surrounded by, a tribe of primitive hunters and food gatherers, for instance, deals with relatively few things: a few tools, a few nets and weapons for hunting, hardly any cloth, some jewelry and pots, but no fixed shelters. Food had to be eaten quickly in order not to become spoiled.

As against the number of *things* a person is involved with (or simply surrounded by) is to be considered the weight of his *doings*. Of course he feels, sees, and hears, because his organism is so constructed that he has virtually no other choice. He sees an animal that he can kill for food, he hears a noise that warns him of a danger; hearing and seeing serve a biological purpose, that of survival. But man not only hears in order to survive; he can also hear as an "extravagance," biologically speaking, serving no specific biological purpose, except the general aim of increased life energy, well-being, aliveness. When he hears in this nonpurposeful way, we say that he *listens*. He listens to the birds' songs, to the raindrops' patter, a human voice's warm timbre, a drum's exciting rhythm, a song's melody, a Bach concerto. Hearing becomes transbiological—humanized, active, creative, "free"—rather than a merely biologically necessary response.

The same is true of seeing. When we see the beautiful ornaments of even the oldest clay vessel, the movement of animals and men in a cave painting from 30,000 years ago, the radiance of a loving face, as well as the horror of the destructiveness done by a human hand, we also have shifted our inner gears from the biologically necessary act to the realm of freedom; from "animal" to "human" existence. The same holds true for our other senses: tasting, touching, smelling. If I need to eat because my body requires food, the usual symptom of this need is *hunger*. If one wants to eat because one enjoys tasty food, one speaks, rather, of *appetite*. Exquisite food is as much a product of cultural development as are music and painting. With smelling it is not different. (Phylogenetically, smelling is the primary sense of orientation for animals just as seeing is for men.) The enjoyment of pleasing smells, as for instance in perfumes, is an old human discovery; it is in the sector of luxury and not in that of biological necessity. Less clearly discernible, but undoubtedly present, is the same difference with regard to touching. Perhaps I have only to remind the reader about people who touch others as they touch a piece of cloth in order to appreciate its quality, as against those whose touch is warm and tender.

The difference between biological necessity and instinctive urge (they complement each other) on the one hand and joyous free exercise of the senses on the other can be recognized clearly in the sexual act, in which all the senses participate. Sex can be the uncultivated expression of biological necessity—i.e., driven, unfree, and undifferentiated excitement. And it can be free, joyous, active, a true luxury not serving any biological purpose. The difference to which I allude here is that between two kinds of doing: passive, driven doing and active, productive, creative doing. Later on, this difference will be discussed at greater length.

At this point I want to stress that while the sector of *things* is immensely smaller for the primitive hunter than it is for cybernetic man, the sector of *human activity* does not show any such discrepancy. In fact, there are good reasons to assume that primitive man *did* more and *was* more than industrial man. Let us have a short look at his situation.

To begin with, all physical work that had to be done he did himself. He had no slaves who worked for him, women were not an exploited class, he had no machines nor even animals to do work for him. He depended on himself, and nobody but himself, as far as physical work was concerned. But, so will the standard objection run, this held true for his physical activities; with regard to thinking, observing, imagining, painting, speculating philosophically and religiously, prehistoric man was far behind man of the machine age. This objection seems valid because we are influenced by the idea that increased schooling is commensurate with increased intellectual and artistic activity. But this is by no means so. Our education is not conducive to increased thinking or the development of active imagination.[1]

The average man today thinks very little for himself. He remembers data as presented by the schools and the mass media; he knows practically nothing of what he knows by his own observing or thinking. Nor does his use of things require much thought or skill. One type of gadget requires no skill or effort at all, as for instance the telephone. Another type of gadget, the automobile, requires some initial learning and after a while, when it has become routine, only a very small amount of personal effort or skill is needed. Nor does modern man—including the educated groups—think much about religious, philosophical, or

---

1. Cf. the radical critique of the school system by I. Illich, *Deschooling Society* (New York: Harper and Row, 1970).

even political problems. He ordinarily adopts one or the other of the many clichés offered him by political or religious books or speakers, but the conclusions are not arrived at as a result of active and penetrating thinking of his own. He chooses the cliché that appeals most to his own character and social class.

Primitive man is in an entirely different situation. He has very little education, in the modern sense of spending a certain amount of time in an educational institution. He himself is forced to observe and to learn from his observations. He observes the weather, the behavior of animals, the behavior of other human beings; his life depends on acquiring certain skills and he acquires them by his own doing and acting, not in "20 quick lessons." His life is a constant process of learning. W. S. Laughlin has given a succinct picture of the primitive hunter's wide range of mental activities:

> There is ample documentation, though surprisingly few systematic studies, for the postulate that primitive man is sophisticated in his knowledge of the natural world. This sophistication encompasses the entire macroscopic zoological world of mammals, marsupials, reptiles, birds, fish, insects, and plants. Knowledge of tides, meteorological phenomena generally, astronomy, and other aspects of the natural world are also well developed among some variations between groups with reference to the sophistication and extent of their knowledge, and to the areas in which they have concentrated . . . I will here only cite the relevance of this sophistication to the hunting behavior system and to its significance for the evolution of man . . . man, the hunter, was learning animal behavior and anatomy, including his own. He domesticated himself first and then turned to other animals and to plants. In this sense, hunting was the school of learning that made the human species self-taught. (W. S. Laughlin, 1968.)

Another example for a distorted evaluation of civilized man's mental activity is the art of reading and writing. Contemporary man believes that to master this art is an unquestionable sign of progress. The greatest efforts are made to eradicate analphabetism, almost as if it were a sign of a mental defect; the progress of a nation is measured—aside from the number of automobiles—by the percentage of people who can read and write. Such value judgments ignore the fact that peoples among whom the art of reading and writing is only the monopoly of small groups of priests or scholars, or does not exist at all, have extraordinary memories. Modern man finds it difficult to understand that a whole literature such as the Vedas, the Buddhist texts, the books of the Old Testament, the later Jewish Oral Tradition were transmitted faithfully from generation to generation, for many hundreds of years, before they were written down. On the contrary, I have observed among people—for instance, Mexican peasants—that even if they can read and write, but do not do so very frequently, the memory is especially good, *because* they do not write down things.

Everyone can make a similar observation with himself. As soon as he writes something down, he ceases to make the act an effort, which memorizing requires. He does not have to engrave, as it were, the data in his brain, because he has stored them in an auxiliary instrument: parchment, paper, or tape. He feels that he does not need to remember, because the content is safely deposited in the notes he has made. The faculty of memory thus suffers from a lack of practice. Today one can observe how people want to avoid active thinking even in small doses: For instance when a salesperson in a store adds up three figures on the machine rather than do them herself.

The same principle of greater activity by primitive man can be seen in art. The primitive hunters and food gatherers, about 30,000 years ago, painted the extraordinary scenes of animals and men, a few of which have come to us well preserved in caves of southern France and northern Spain. These beautiful paintings are a delight even for modern man, who is familiar with the painting of the great masters of the last several centuries. But even if we would say that the cave painters were geniuses (the Da Vincis and Rembrandts of the last Ice Age), this can hardly be said for the ornamentation of pottery and tools, dating back to the oldest prehistorical times. It has often been said that the cave paintings, as well as these ornaments, had practical, magic purposes such as to contribute to the success of the hunt, to fight evil spirits, and so on. But, even granted this, whatever the practical purposes may have been, it was not required that things be made so beautiful. Besides, the ornamentation of the pottery cannot have been the creation of so many geniuses. That every village had its own style of ornament—often varying only slightly—proves that these people had an active aesthetic interest.

I have spoken so far of the most "primitive" cultures, the primitive hunters and food gatherers, and what we know and can surmise of their cultures, at least since the full emergence of *homo sapiens sapiens* around 40,000 to 50,000 years ago. They made few things with their hands, yet they were very active in applying their own faculties of thinking, observing, imagining, painting, and sculpting. If one wanted to express the relation between the "thing sector" to the "doing sector" in quantitative terms, one could state that among the most primitive people it is $1:100$, whereas the proportion for modern man would be $100:1$.[2]

History offers us many variations between these two extremes. A Greek citizen in the period of the flowering of Greek democracy was certainly surrounded by more things than the hunter, yet he was actively concerned with the affairs of state, he developed and used his reason to an extraordinary degree, he was engaged, both artistically and philosophically. What more do we have to know of a population than that the dramas of Sophocles and Aeschylus formed the artistic nurture of an Athenian citizen, and what does it say about the aesthetic and emotional passivity of a contemporary New Yorker, if we think of the plays and movies that excite him!

Different and yet in many ways similar is the picture we get from the life of a medieval artisan. His work was done with interest, with care, it was not boring; the making of a table was a creative act in which the table was the child of his efforts, his experience, his skill, and his taste. Most of what had to be done he had to do himself. He was also actively engaged in many

---

2. These figures should only express *symbolically* the quantitative relation between the two sectors.

common activities, such as singing, dancing, and church services. The peasant was much worse off materially: He was not a free man, yet he was not quite a slave either. The work in the fields may not have given much satisfaction (I speak here especially of the period before the position of the peasant deteriorated considerably in the sixteenth century), yet he participated in and enjoyed a culturally rich life based on his specific folk culture. Neither he nor the artisan were spoonfed by seeing *others* making efforts, or enjoying themselves, or suffering. Whatever filled their lives, it was largely a result of their own doing and their own experience. Even the artisan, economically and socially far superior to the peasant, did not *have* much, except his house and his tools, and he earned just enough to live according to the traditional standard of living of his social class. He did not want to have or to consume more, because not the acquisition of riches but the productive use of his faculties and the enjoyment of being were his goal.

Contemporary man, in cybernetic society, is surrounded by as many *things* as there are stars in the sky. To be sure, he has produced most of them. But has "he"? The worker in a giant factory produces—no-thing. Surely he participates in the production of an automobile, or an electric refrigerator, or a toothpaste, but, depending on the kind of industrial process, he makes a few stereotyped movements, puts in some screws, or the motor or a door. Only the final worker in the chain sees the finished product; the others see it on the streets—they acquire and own a cheaper car, they see only the expensive car driven by people who are better off. But that the single worker has produced a car can be said only in an abstract sense. In the first place, machines have produced the car (and other machines have produced the car-producing machines); the worker—not as a full man but as an alive tool—has a part in the production in the performance of tasks that cannot yet be done by machines (or only too expensively).

The engineer and stylist may claim that *they* have produced the car; but surely that is not true; they may have contributed their share, but *they* have not produced the car. Eventually, the executive, or manager, will claim that *he* has produced the car;

he thinks that because he directed the whole process, he has produced the car. But this claim is even more dubious than that of the engineer. We do not know whether the manager was, as a physical entity, really necessary for the production of the car. His claim may be as questionable as that of a general who insists that *he* conquered a fortress or won a battle when quite obviously his soldiers conquered the fortress and fought the battle; *they* moved, attacked, were wounded or killed, while he had made the plans and saw to their proper execution. Sometimes the battle is won because the opposing general is simply more incapable than the winning one, and thus the victory is won by the faults of the opponent. The problem here is that of the productive role of the directing and managing function, which I shall not further pursue except to say that, for the manager, the car has been transformed from the physical appearance of the car as it leaves the assembly line into a commodity; this means the car to him is not primarily interesting because of its real use value, but because of its fictitious use value suggested by advertising that bamboozles the mind of the prospective buyer with all sorts of irrelevant data—from sexy girls to "virile"-looking cars. The car as a commodity is in a sense the product of the manager, who orders the real car to be made with profit-pregnant features that can give it special sales appeal.

Modern man can produce effects in the material world that are greater than earlier man ever was able to achieve. But these effects are completely incommensurate with the physical and intellectual efforts invested in them. To drive a powerful automobile requires neither physical strength nor particular skill or intelligence. To fly an airplane requires a great deal of skill; to drop a hydrogen bomb, relatively little. To be sure, there are some activities that still require considerable skill and effort: those of artisans, physicians, scientists, artists, highly skilled workers, pilots, fishermen, horticulturists, and some other such occupations or professions. Yet these skill-requiring activities are increasingly fewer; the vast majority of men make a living by work that requires little intelligence, imagination, or concentration of any kind. Physical effects (results) are no longer proportionate to human effort, and this *separation between effort (and skill) and result* is one of the most significant and pathogenic features of modern society, because it tends to degrade effort and to minimize its significance.

We must arrive, then, at a first conclusion: In contrast to the generally accepted view, modern man is basically very helpless in relation to his world. He only appears powerful because he dominates nature to an extraordinary degree. But this domination is almost completely alienated; it is not the result of his real human powers but of the "megamachine,"[3] which enables him to achieve much without doing much or being much.

Thus, modern man can be said to live in a symbiotic relationship with the world of machines. Inasmuch as he is a part of them, he is—or appears to be—powerful. Without them, standing by himself, using his own resources, he is as powerless as a little child. That is why he worships his machines: They lend him their strength, they create the illusion that he is a giant, when without them he is a cripple. When man in other ages believed that his idols gave him his strength, it was pure illusion, except that he projected his strength into the idol and received some of it back in the worship of it. In the worship of the machines it is basically the same. To be sure, Baal and Astarte were only what man *thought* they were; the idols were, as prophetic critique put it, nothing but pieces of wood or stone, and their power was exclusively that of man's having transferred his own power to them and getting part of that power back from them. Machines, however, are not mere ineffective pieces of metal; they do create a world of useful things. Man is *really* dependent on them. But just as with the idols, it is he who has invented, planned, and built them; they, like the idols, are the product of his imagination, of his technical imagination, which, coupled with science, has been able to create things which are realistically very effective—yet which have become his ruler.

According to legend, Prometheus brought man fire, in order

---

3. Lewis Mumford coined this term; cf. his *The Myth of the Machine: Techniques and Human Development* (New York: Harcourt, Brace and World, 1967).

to liberate him from the control by nature. Man at this point of his history has enslaved himself to the very fire that was to liberate him. Man today, wearing the mask of a giant, has become a weak, helpless being dependent on the machines *he* made, and hence on the leaders who guarantee the proper functioning of the society that produces the machines, dependent on a well-functioning business, frightened to death of losing all the props, of being "a man without rank and without title," of just being, of being challenged by the question "Who am I?"

In summary, modern man *has* many things and uses many things, but he *is* very little. His feelings and thinking processes are atrophied like unused muscles. He is afraid of any crucial social change because any disturbance in the social balance to him spells chaos or death—if not physical death, the death of his identity.

15. On the Philosophy of Having

That which one *has* is one's *property,* and inasmuch as everybody "has" his body it could be argued that property is rooted in the very physical existence of man. But even though this would appear to be a good argument for the universality of property, it hardly serves this purpose, because it is not correct: A slave does *not* own his body; it can be used, sold, destroyed, according to his owner's will and whim. The slave, in this respect, differs from even the most exploited worker; the latter does not own his body energy because he is forced to sell it to the owner of capital who buys his working power. (However, since he has no choice, under the conditions of capitalism, one must admit that even his ownership of his body is questionable.) What does it mean that I own something when somebody else owns the right to use what I have?

We are here in the middle of a much-disputed problem, in which still a great deal of confusion exists, that of *property*. A clear understanding of property has been greatly obscured by the passionate feelings related to the revolutionary demands for abolition of private property. Many people have thought that their personal property—their clothes, books, furniture, and so on, even their spouses—would be taken away and "nationalized"[1] (Of course, the swingers today have, in fact, begun to "socialize" their wives, among each other, although otherwise sharing politically conservative views.)

Marx and other socialists had never proposed anything as silly as that the personal property or things one uses should be socialized; they were referring to the ownership of capital—i.e., the means of production that enable an owner to produce commodities that were socially undesirable and to impose on the worker his conditions because he, the owner, "gave" him work.

As a reaction against socialist demands, the professors in political economy asserted that property was a "natural" right, inherent in human nature, and that it had existed as long as human society. Attending several courses on economic history in 1918 and 1919, I heard two (at the time) outstanding professors lecture, in all seriousness, that capital was not characteristic of capitalism alone, but that even the primitive tribes who used cowrie shells as means of exchange thus proved that they had capital—ergo, that capitalism was as old as mankind. Their example from primitive peoples was actually badly chosen. We know now, even better, that the most primitive peoples had no private property, except in the things that served their immediate personal needs, such as cloth, jewelry, tools, nets, arms, and weapons. In fact, most of the classical accounts of the origin and function of private property have taken for granted that in nature all things were held in common (the views of anthropologists I have presented in *The Anatomy of Human Destructiveness*). Even the Church Fathers indirectly accepted this view. According to them, property was both the consequence and the social remedy for the sin of covetousness that came with the Fall of Man; in other

---

1. I still remember vividly my shock at the fantastic report of the *Frankfurter Zeitung,* in many ways an equivalent of the *New York Times,* from Munich in 1919 that Gustav Landauer, one of the finest humanists of Germany, and at the time minister of culture of the short-lived Bavarian Räterepublik, had ordered the nationalization of women!

words, private property was a result of the Fall, just as was
male domination over women and the conflict between man and
nature.

It is useful to distinguish between various concepts of property
that are sometimes confused. First there is the view of property
as an absolute right over an object (living or non-living) regardless of whether the owner has done anything to produce it, or
whether he inherited it, received it as a gift or inheritance, or
acquired it by theft. Aside from the latter point, which requires
certain qualifications both in the relations between nations and
the laws in civil society, the great law systems of Rome and of
the modern state speak of property in this sense. Possession is
always guaranteed by national or international law, i.e., fundamentally by the violence that "enforces" the law. A second concept, particularly popular in the philosophy of the eighteenth-
century Enlightenment, stresses that one's title to possess something depends on the effort one has made to create it. Characteristic is John Locke's view that if one adds one's labor to
something that, at this point, is nobody's property *(res nullius)*
it becomes one's own property. But Locke's emphasis on one's
productive part in establishing property, originally, loses most
of its significance by his additional qualification that the title to
property one has established could be freely transferred to others
who had not worked for it. Locke apparently needed this qualification because otherwise he would have run into the difficulty
that workers could claim the products of their work as *their*
property.[2]

A third concept of property, which transcends the aforemen-
tioned essentially legal concepts and is based on the meaning of
property for man, metaphysically and spiritually, comes from
those promulgated by Hegel and Marx. For Hegel [in his *Philosophy of Right,* Sections 41 and 45] property was necessary because
"a person must translate his freedom into an external sphere in

---

2. Cf. Stanley I. Bern, article on "Property"; in Paul Edwards (ed.), *The
Encyclopedia of Philosophy* (New York: Macmillan Comp. and the Free Press,
1967).

order that he may achieve his ideal existence," since property was "the first embodiment of freedom and so is in itself a substantive end." While Hegel's statement may sound, at superficial reading, to be nothing but a rationalization for the sacredness of private property, it is indeed much more, although space does not permit an exposition of Hegel's philosophy that is necessary for a full understanding. Marx formulated the problem entirely *ad personam* and without any philosophical mystification. As with Hegel, property was for him an externalization of the human will. But as long as the property created was not his but the owner's of the means of production, as long as man was alienated from his own work, property could not be *his* property. Only when society was organized in a common enterprise, where the full development of the individual depended on the full development of all, "mine" or "thine" were meaningless concepts. In such a community, labor itself—i.e., unalienated labor[3]—would become pleasureful and "possession," aside from objects that one used, an absurdity. Everybody would receive not according to the amount of work he did, but according to his needs. (Needs here, of course, real needs of man and not synthetic, damaging needs suggested to him by industry.)

A radically different distinction is that between property for use (functional property), and property for possession (nonfunctional), although there are many blendings of these two types. In German the difference between the two kinds of properties is made clear by the use of two different words: *Besitz* and *Eigentum. Besitz* comes from *sitzen,* and means literally that upon which one sits; it refers to that which one controls, legally and factually, but it is not related to one's own productive action. *Eigentum,* on the other hand, is different. While *aig* is the Germanic root of *haben* (to have), it has changed its meaning in the course of many centuries so that Meister Eckhart could translate

---

3. Marx's attitude toward unalienated labor remains contradictory; sometimes he seems to consider unalienated labor the highest achievement of life, but his final conclusion is that free time and the unalienated use of it are the supreme goal of life.

it already in the thirteenth century as the German equivalent of the Latin word for property *(proprietas)*. *Proper* corresponds to *eigen;* it means that which is particular of a person (as in "proper name"). *Eigentum = proprietas =* property refers then, to all that is particular of a person as a specific individual: his own body, the things that he uses daily, and to which he gives some of his individuality by this daily acquaintance, even his tools and abode—all that forms his constant surroundings.

It is perhaps difficult for a person living in today's cybernetic society, in which everything is obsolete in a short time (and even if it is not, it will eventually be exchanged for something newer), to appreciate the personal character of the things of daily use. In using them one imparts something of his life and of his personality to them. They are not lifeless, sterile, or changeable things anymore. That this is true has been clearly demonstrated in the custom of many earlier cultures (by no means only primitive) to put in a person's grave the very things of his personal and daily property. The equivalent in modern society is a person's last will and testament, which may have its consequences for years after his death. But his objects are not his personal things, but precisely the impersonal private property, he owned such as money, land, rights, and so forth.

We can conclude, then, that the most fundamental difference is that between *personal* and *private* property, which essentially is the same as that between *functional* and *nonfunctional* (dead) property.

This difference is by far more fundamental than that between private and public property, since, as many examples have shown, the legal form of a public, or national, or socialized property can be just as coercive and alienating as private property, provided it is managed by bureaucrats who only in name but not in fact represent the interests of the workers and employees.

Functional and dead property appear often in their pure form, but they are frequently blended, as we can easily see in the following examples. The most elementary example is the body.

The body is the only property everybody has; it is, as it were, a "natural property." For the infant, as Freud has so brilliantly shown, the excrements are probably experienced as a still more extreme form of possession. They are *his*, the product of his body, he gets rid of them but need not fear this loss too much because every day replenishes the loss of the previous day. But the body, in contrast, is not *only* a "possession"; it is also an instrument, which we use to satisfy our needs, and furthermore it changes according to the use we make of it. If we do not use our muscles, they become weaker, flabbier, even to the extreme point of becoming unusable. On the contrary, our body becomes stronger and healthier the more it is used (of course within certain limits).

In the case of having a house or a piece of land the situation is different, because we deal here with a social category and not with a natural one, as is the case with the body. Let us think of a nomadic tribe: They did not *own* land; they lived on a piece of land for a while, used it, built their tents or huts on it, and after a while abandoned it. The land was not their private property, nor was it communal property—it was not property at all, but an object of use that was "theirs" only in the very restricted sense that they used it. The same holds true for tools, such as fishing nets, spears, axes, and so on; they were possessions only inasmuch as they were used. The same principle exists in certain agricultural cooperatives today, where the individual does not *own* land, i.e., where he cannot sell it and has a right to it only as long and to the extent to which he cultivates it.

Among many primitive cultures without private property, the same principle applies to the relationship of man to woman and to the institution of marriage. A relationship is socially recognized as marriage as long as the man and the woman love each other, want each other, and want to stay together. When the relationship loses this function, each one is free to leave, because no one has the other.[4]

In contrast, with regard to institutional property, the law

---

4. An example is the marriage among the African Pygmies, the Mbutus. Cf. C. Turnbull, *Wayward Servants, or The Two Worlds of the African Pygmies* (London: Eyre & Spottiswoode, 1965).

states that my house or my land, or my tools or my wife or my children are my property; that I *have* them and it does not matter whether I care for them. In fact, it is my right to destroy everything that is my property: I can burn my house, or a painting even if it is a unique work of art. I do not owe an account to anybody for what I do with what is mine. This legal right is effective because the state supports my claim with its power.

In the course of history the concepts of property rights over wives and children and the corresponding laws have changed. Today to kill one's wife is a crime that is punished as murder. To kill one's child is also considered a crime, but endless cruelties and brutalities by which parents assault their children is within the exercise of their legitimate authority (i.e., property rights) unless it goes to extremes that cannot be ignored. Nevertheless, in one's relationship to his wife and children there have always been elements transcending pure possession. They were living beings, they were living in close contact with their master, he needed them and they gave him pleasure; hence, there was also an element of functional property in addition to legal property.

Property in the form of capital is the extreme form of legal possession-property. It could be said that capital is not different from a tool, for instance an ax, that its owner uses. But in the case of the ax it becomes valuable only by its serving its owner's skill, i.e., as functional property. In the case of capital, the owner *has* it—even if he does nothing with it. It remains valuable even if it is not invested; but if the owner invests it, he does not have to use his skill or make any commensurate effort to bring him profit. The same holds true for the oldest form of capital: Land. My legal right that makes me the owner permits me to gain profit from it without making any effort, i.e., without doing any work myself. It is for this reason that nonfunctional property may also be called dead property.

"Dead," or nonfunctional, property has its legitimacy in conquest, or in law. But the law itself is backed up by force, and in this sense the difference between conquered property and legal property is only relative. Also, in the case of legal possession *force constitutes right,* because the state guarantees my property right by force, of which the state has the monopoly.

*   *   *

Man cannot exist without "having," but he can exist very well with purely *functional* having and has existed so for the first ± 40,000 years of his history since he emerged as *homo sapiens sapiens.* Indeed, he can, as I shall argue later, *only* exist sanely if he has mainly functional property and a minimum of dead property. Functional property is an existential and actual need of man; institutional property satisfies pathological need, conditioned by certain socio-economic circumstances. Man must have a body, shelter, tools, weapons, vessels. These things are necessary for his biological existence; there are other things that he needs for his spiritual existence, such as ornaments and objects of decoration—briefly, artistic and "sacred" objects and the means to produce them. They can be property in the sense that an individual uses them exclusively, but they are functional property.

With an increase in civilization, functional property in things increases. The individual may have several suits or dresses, a house, labor-saving devices, radio and television machines, record players and recordings, books, tennis rackets, a pair of skis. . . . All these possessions need not be different from those functional possessions that exist in primitive cultures. They need not be, but they often are. The change of function happens at the point where possession ceases to be an instrument for greater aliveness and productivity but is transformed into a means for passive–receptive consumption. When having has primarily the function of satisfying the need for ever-increasing consumption, it ceases to be a condition for more being but is basically no different from "keeping-possession." This statement may sound strange since "keeping" and "spending" are opposites. This is so indeed, if we look only at the surface. But seen dynamically, they share one fundamental quality: The miser as well as the waster is inwardly passive and unproductive. Neither is actively related to anything or anybody, neither changes and grows in the process of living; each only represents one of two different forms of nonaliveness. Showing the distinction between possession-having and use-having needs to take into account the double meaning of use: Passive use ("the consumer") and productive use (the artisan, artist, skilled worker). Functional having refers to productive use.

Also, "possessive having" can have another function than that of gaining without having to make an effort. In the first place, dead property gives power to its owner in a society centered around property. The one who has much property is usually politically powerful; he appears to be a great man because he is a powerful man; people admire his greatness because they prefer to admire to being afraid. The rich and powerful man can influence others by intimidating them or by buying them; hence, he acquires the possession of fame or admiration.

Marx has given a beautiful analysis of this last point:

> That which exists for me through the medium of *money*, that which I can pay for (i.e., which money can buy), that *I am*, the possessor of the money. My own power is as great as the power of money. The properties of money are my own (the possessor's) properties and faculties. What I *am* and *can do* is, therefore, not at all determined by my individuality. I *am* ugly, but I can buy the *most beautiful woman* for myself. Consequently, I am not *ugly*, for the effect of *ugliness*, its power to repel, is annulled by money. As an individual I am *lame*, but money provides me with twenty-four legs. Therefore, I am not lame. I am a detestable, dishonorable, unscrupulous and stupid man, but money is honored and so also is its possessor. Money is the highest good, and so its possessor is good. Besides, money saves me the trouble of being dishonest; therefore, I am presumed honest. I am *stupid*, but since money is the *real mind* of all things, how should its possessor be stupid? Moreover, he can buy talented people for himself, and is not he who has power over the talented more talented than they? I who can have, through the power of money, *everything* for which the human heart longs, do I not possess all human abilities? Does not my money, therefore, transform all my incapacities into their opposites?
>
> If *money* is the bond which binds me to *human* life, and society

to me, and which links me with nature and man, is it not the bond of all *bonds*? Is it not, therefore also the universal agent of separation? It is the real means of both *separation* and *union*, the galvano-*chemical* power of society. . . .

Since money, as the existing and active concept of value, confounds and exchanges everything, it is the universal *confusion and transposition* of all things, the inverted world, the confusion and transposition of all natural and human qualities.

He who can purchase bravery is brave, though a coward. Money is not exchanged for a particular quality, a particular thing, or a specific human faculty, but for the whole objective world of man and nature. Thus, from the standpoint of its possessor, it exchanges every quality and object for every other, even though they are contradictory. It is the fraternization of incompatibles; it forces contraries to embrace.

Let us assume *man* to be *man,* and his relation to the world to be a human one. Then love can only be exchanged for love, trust for trust, etc. If you wish to enjoy art you must be an artistically cultivated person; if you wish to influence other people you must be a person who really has a stimulating and encouraging effect upon others. Every one of your relations to man and to nature must be a *specific expression,* corresponding to the object of your will, of your *real individual* life. If you love without evoking love in return, i.e., if you are not able, by the *manifestation* of yourself as a loving person, to make yourself a *beloved person,* then your love is impotent and a misfortune.[5]

These considerations lead to the conclusion that the conventional classification of property in private and public (nationalized or socialized) property is insufficient and even misleading. What matters most is whether the property is functional, and hence nonexploitative, or whether it is dead, exploitative property. Even if the property belongs to the state, or even if it belongs to all those who work in the factory, it may give the command over others to the bureaucrats who control production. In fact, purely functional property such as objects for use

---

5. *Economic and Philosophical Manuscripts 1844,* in E. Fromm, *Marx's Concept of Man* (New York: Frederick Ungar, 1961).

were never considered by Marx and other socialists as private property that should be socialized. Nor does it matter whether the functional property is exactly equal for everybody. This concern with equality of property was never one of the socialists'; it is, in actuality, deeply rooted in the spirit of property that, engendering envy, looks for the avoidance of any inequality because it would generate envy.

The central issue is whether possession furthers the activity and aliveness of an individual, or whether it paralyzes his activity and furthers indolence, sloth, and unproductivity.

16. On the Psychology of Having

With this last remark we enter into the discussion of *having* as a mental and affective phenomenon.

Speaking about "functional property" first, it is clear that I can own no more than I can reasonably use. This coupling of owning and using has several consequences: (1) My activity is constantly stimulated, because having only what I use, I am constantly stimulated to be active; (2) The greediness to possess (avarice) can hardly develop, because I can only wish to have the amount of things that fit my capacity to use them productively; (3) I can hardly develop envy since it would be useless to envy another for what he has when I am busy using what I have; and (4) I am not worried by the fear of losing what I have, since functional property is easily replaceable.

Institutional possession is an entirely different experience. It is—aside from functional having and being—the other elementary mode of experience of oneself and the world. These two modes of experience are to be found in almost everybody: Rare are those who do not experience having at all, far more numerous are those for whom it is almost the only experience they know. Most people are characterized by the particular blending of the having and being modes in their character structure. Yet, simple as the concept and word *having* seems to be, to describe the experience of the having mode is difficult, especially because such a description can succeed only if the reader responds not only intellectually but tries to mobilize his affective experience with having.

Perhaps the most helpful approach to the understanding of having (in the nonfunctional sense) is to recall one of the most significant insights of Freud. He found that after the infant goes through a phase of mere passive receptivity, followed by one of aggressive, exploitative receptivity, the child, before it reaches maturity, goes through a phase that Freud designated as the anal erotic phase, which often remains dominant in the development of a person and leads to the development of the "anal character." In this context, it is of little importance that Freud believed a special phase of the libido development was primary and that character formation was secondary (whereas in my opinion as well in that of authors closer to Freud, like Erik Erikson, the relation is in the reverse); what matters is the view that the predominant orientation toward possession is seen by Freud as the period before the achievement of full maturity and as pathological if it remains permanent. In other words, for Freud the person exclusively concerned with having and possession is a neurotic, mentally sick person.

This point of view may have been a bombshell within a society that is based on private property and whose members experienced themselves and their relationship to the world predominantly in terms of possession. Yet, as far as I know, no one protested against this attack on the highest values of bourgeois society, while Freud's modest attempts to de-demonize sex were met with a howl by all defenders of "decency." It is not easy to explain this paradox. Was the reason that scarcely anybody connected individual psychology with social psychology? Was it that the supreme moral value of ownership was so undisputed that nobody picked up the challenge? Or was it that Freud's attack on middle-class sexual morals was so bitterly scorned because the attack served as a defense against one's own hypocrisy, while the public's attitude toward money and possessions was completely genuine and no aggressive defense was needed?

However this may be, there is no doubt that Freud believed

that possessiveness as such—i.e., having—was an unhealthful orientation, if it was dominant in an adult person.

He brought to bear several kinds of data to establish his theory—first of all, those rich data in which excrements were symbolically equated with money, possession, and dirt. There is indeed ample linguistic, folkloric, and mythical data to bear this out. Freud had already in a letter to Fliess of December 22, 1897,[1] associated money and miserliness with feces. In his classic paper, "Character and Analeroticism" (1908) he added more examples to this symbolic identity:

> The connections between the complexes of interest in money and of defaecation, which seem so dissimilar, appear to be the most extensive of all. Every doctor who has practiced psychoanalysis knows that the most refractory and long-standing cases of what is described as habitual constipation in neurotics can be cured by that form of treatment. This is less surprising if we remember that that function has shown itself similarly amenable to hypnotic suggestion. But in psychoanalysis one only achieves this result if one deals with the patients' money complex and induces them to bring it into consciousness with all its connections. It might be supposed that the neurosis is here only following an indication of common usage in speech, which calls a person who keeps too careful a hold on his money "dirty" or "filthy." But this explanation would be far too superficial. In reality, wherever archaic modes of thought have predominated or persist—in the ancient civilizations, in myths, fairy tales and superstitions, in unconscious thinking, in dreams and in neuroses—money is brought into the most intimate relationship with dirt. We know that the gold which the devil gives his paramours turns into excrement after his departure, and the devil is certainly nothing else than the personification of the repressed unconscious instinctual life. We also know about the superstition which connects the finding of treasure with defaecation, and everyone is familiar with the figure of the "shitter of ducats" *(Dukatenscheisser)*. Indeed, even according to ancient Babylonian doctrine gold is "the feces

---

1. Letter 79, *Standard Edition of the Complete Psychological Works of Sigmund Freud* (S.E.), vol. 1 (London: Hogarth Press, 1966), pp. 272–73.

of Hell" (Mammon = ilu mamman). Thus in following the usage of language, neurosis, here as elsewhere, is taking words in their original, significant sense, and where it appears to be using a word figuratively it is usually simply restoring its old meaning.

It is possible that the contrast between the most precious substance known to men and the most worthless, which they reject as waste matter ("refuse"), has led to this specific identification of gold with faeces.[2]

A few words of comment are indicated. In the Babylonian notion that gold is "the feces of Hell," the connection is made between gold, feces, and death. In Hell, meaning the world of the dead, the most valuable object is feces and this brings together the notion of money, dirt, and the dead.[3]

The last of the two paragraphs quoted here is very revealing of Freud's dependency on the thinking of his day. Seeking the reason for the symbolic identity of gold and feces, he proposes the hypothesis that their identity may be based on the very fact of their radical contrast, gold being the most precious and feces the most worthless substance known to man. Freud ignores the other possibility that gold is the most precious substance for civilization, whose economy is (generally) based on gold, but that this holds by no means for those primitive societies for which gold may not have had any great value. More importantly, while the pattern of his society suggests that man think of gold as the most precious substance, he may unconsciously carry a notion that gold is dead, sterile (like salt), without life (except when used in jewelry); that it is amassed labor, meant to be hoarded, the foremost example of possession without function. Can one eat gold? Can one make anything grow with gold (except when it has been transformed into capital)? This dead, sterile aspect of gold is shown in the myth of King Midas. He was so avaricious that his wish was granted that everything he touched became

---

2. Freud's Collected Papers, S.E. vol. 9 (1908). This connection is important in connection with the phenomenon of necrophilia. Cf. E. Fromm, *The Anatomy of Human Destructiveness*.

3. Ibid.

gold. Eventually, he had to die precisely because one cannot live from gold. In this myth is a clear vision of the sterility of gold, and it is by no means the highest value, as Freud assumed. Freud was too much a son of his time to be aware of the negative value of money and possession and, hence, of the critical implications of his concept of the anal character, which I discussed above.

Regardless of the merits of Freud's scheme of libido development, his findings about the receptive and possessive stages as one of the earliest stages of human development make much sense. The first years in the child's life are necessarily a period during which the infant is not capable of taking care of itself, to form the surrounding world according to its wishes under its own powers. It is forced either to receive, to snatch, or to possess because it cannot yet produce. Thus, the category of having is a necessary transitional stage in the child's development. But if possessiveness remains the dominant experience in the adult, it indicates that he has not achieved the goal of normal development to productivity but has become stuck in the experience of having, because of this failure in his development. Here, as with other orientations, what is normal at an early stage of evolution becomes pathological if it occurs at a later stage. Possessive having is based on the reduction of the capacity for productive activity. This reduction can be traced to many factors. By productive activity, I understand the free, active expression of one's faculties, *not* the actions motivated by instincts or by the compulsive need to act in certain ways. This is not the place to take up this discussion. Suffice it to say here that we must look for factors such as early intimidation, lack of stimulation, over-pampering, both individually and socially. But the sequence also goes the other way around; the having orientation and its satisfaction weakens the effort and eventually the capacity to make productive efforts. The more a person *has,* the less is he attracted to making active efforts.[4] Having and inner laziness ultimately form a vicious circle, reinforcing each other.

---

4. For a full discussion see E. Fromm, *The Anatomy of Human Destructiveness.*

*   *   *

Let us look at an example of a person whose total orientation is one of having: The *miser*. The most obvious object of possession for him is money and its material equivalents such as land, houses, movable property, etc. Most of his energy is directed toward keeping it, more by saving and non-use rather than by business activities and speculation. He experiences himself as if he were a fortress; nothing must leave it, hence, nothing must be spent beyond what is absolutely necessary. And what this "absolutely necessary" is depends on the degree of his miserliness.

It is exceptional though not rare that a person would deprive himself of all amenities of life, such as pleasant food, nice clothing, and decent housing, in order to reduce his expenses to almost nothing. The average person is puzzled why a person should deprive himself of all enjoyments. But one must not forget that this is not really the case; the miser finds the greatest enjoyment precisely in the experience of his possession; "to have" is for him a sweeter pleasure than beauty, love, or any sensuous or intellectual pleasure. The rich miser presents a picture that is sometimes less obvious. He may even spend millions in philanthropy or for art because it is an expense that (aside from tax advantages) is demanded by his social status and because of the publicity value of a favorable image. But he may go to great lengths to set up a control system that insures him against any unnecessary expenditure of postage, or he may make compulsive efforts to prevent his workers' losing even one minute of their working time. (Bennet even reports that Henry Ford, the founder of the automobile dynasty, wore socks until they could hardly be mended any more, and being afraid of his wife secretly buying new socks in a store, changed them in his car and threw away the old ones on the way.)

The miser is not only driven by the passion to save things, but equally by that of saving energy, feelings, thought, or anything else that one can "have." For him energy is a fixed amount which he has, and which cannot be replenished. Hence, every expenditure of energy that is not absolutely necessary must be avoided because it diminishes his stock of it. He avoids unnecessary physical efforts, does everything in the shortest possible way. Usually he works out pedantic, orderly methods for maximal reduction of energy consumption. This attitude often becomes manifest in his sexual behavior (this manifestation is obviously to be found mostly among men.) To him, semen is a most precious product, but limited in quantity; whatever is spent of it is lost forever. (That he knows intellectually that this is not so has little effect on the way he feels about it.) Therefore, he must reduce sexual intercourse to a minimum in order to lose only a minimum of semen. I have known quite a number of men who had worked out a system to achieve the optimal compromise between the demands of saving and of "health," which, they thought, demands a certain amount of sexual activity. (This complex is sometimes at the root of male impotence.)

In the same way, the miser tends to save words, feelings, and thoughts. He does not want to spend energy in feeling or thinking; he needs this energy for the necessary and unavoidable tasks of life. He remains cold and indifferent to the joys and sorrows of others, even his own. As a substitute for a live experience he substitutes the memory of past experiences. These memories are a precious possession, and often he goes over them in thought as he would count his money, his cattle, or his industrial stocks. In fact, the memory of past feelings or experiences is the only form in which he is in touch with his own experiences. He is feeling little, but he is *sentimental;* sentimental being used here in the sense of "feelingless feelings," the *thought* of or the *daydreams* of feelings, rather than *felt* feelings. It is a well-known fact that many possessive, cold, and even cruel people—and the three belong together—who are not moved by human suffering that is real, can shed tears when a movie presents one of those constellations that they remember from their own childhood or that they think of in daydreams.

*   *   *

We have so far ignored the differences in the objects possessed along with the respective difference in the experience of possessing them. Probably the most important difference is between nonliving and living objects. Nonliving objects—money, land, and jewelry—do not oppose their owner. The only opposition could come from social and political forces that threaten the safe and secure possession of property. The most important guarantee for this security is the law and the exercise of force by the state, which make it effective. Those whose inner security is by and large based on possession are necessarily conservative and ardent opponents of movements that want to reduce the state's monopoly of force.

For those whose security rests on the possession of living beings, especially of human beings, the situation is more complex. They, too, are dependent on the state's capacity of "enforcing" the law, but they are also confronted with the resistance of the human being to being possessed, to being transformed into a thing that can be *had* and controlled. This statement may be questioned by some: They will point out the fact that millions of people are satisfied with being ruled, in fact that they prefer control to freedom. In *Escape from Freedom* (1941) I attempted myself to point to this "fear of freedom" and to the attraction of unfreedom. But the apparent contradiction is not insoluble. To be free, rather than to *have* security, is frightening to anyone who has not acquired the courage for the adventure of being. He is willing to give up his freedom if his coercion is made to appear as noncoercion, if the controller is given the features of a benign father, if he feels he is not a thing controlled but a loved child guided. But where this disguise is not used and the object of possession is aware of what happens to him, his first reaction is that of resistance, in all forms and with all means. The child resists with the weapons of the helpless: Sabotage and obstruction—more specifically, his weapons are bed-wetting, constipation, temper tantrums, and so on. The helpless classes react sometimes by sabotage or inefficiency but, as history shows, often by frank rebellions and revolutions, which are the birth pains of new developments.

Whatever form the fight against domination takes, it has a deep influence on the one who wants to control. He must develop the passionate striving to control others, and this drive becomes a passion charged with lust. The attempt to possess ("have") human beings necessarily leads to the development of sadism, one of the ugliest and most perverted of passions.

The ultimate object of having is to have *oneself.* "I have myself" means I am full with myself, I am what I have, and I have what I am. The true representative of this type of person is the full-fledged narcissist. He is filled only with himself; he transforms the whole world into something he owns. He is not interested in anything or anybody outside himself, except as objects to be incorporated into his sphere of possessions.

*   *   *

A mode of experience that is fundamentally akin to that of having is consuming. Again we can easily distinguish between functional (rational) and nonfunctional (irrational) consumption.

If I eat because my hunger indicates my body's need for food, or because I enjoy food, my eating is functional and rational,[5] in the sense that it serves the healthful operation of my entire organism, including my educated taste. But if I overeat out of greed, depression, or anxiety, my eating is irrational; it harms, and does not further me physiologically or mentally. This holds true for all consumption, which is rooted in greed and has an obsessional character: In avarice, drug addiction, in the consumerism of today and for sexual consumption. What appears today as a great pleasure-producing sexual passion is actually only an expression of greed, an attempt to devour each other. It is an attempt of two people, or one of two, to take full possession of the other. People sometimes describe their most ardent sexual experiences in words such as "We fell upon each other." Indeed they do, they fall upon each other like hungry wolves, and the basic mood is that of hostile possessiveness and not that of joy—not to speak of love.

To fill oneself up with people, food, or other things is a more archaic form of possession and having. In the latter case the

---

5. Cf. the discussion on rationality in E. Fromm, *The Anatomy of Human Destructiveness.*

object I have can still be taken away from me, by superior force, trickery, and so on. My possession requires a social situation that guarantees my title.

If I introject the object I want to keep, it is safe from all interference. Nobody can rob me of what I have swallowed. This first type of having can be clearly seen in the infant's attempt to take things into its mouth. This is his first way of securely having. But of course, as far as physical objects are concerned, the method of introjection is extremely limited; strictly speaking, it can occur only with objects that are edible and not harmful to the organism. Cannibalism may have one of its roots here: If I believe that the body of a man, especially of a strong and brave man, gives strength, eating it would be the archaic equivalent of acquiring a slave.

But there is a type of consumption that is not necessarily by mouth. The best example is the private automobile. It can be argued that such is functional property and for this reason not equivalent to dead possession. This would be true if the private car were really functional—but it is not. It does not stimulate or activate any of man's powers. It is a distraction, enables a person to run away from himself, produces a false sense of strength, helps to form a sense of identity based on the brand of car the man drives; it prevents him from walking and thinking, is sufficiently exacting to make a concentrated conversation impossible, and stimulates competition. One would need to write a book in order to give a full description of the irrational and pathogenic function of the type of consumption that the private automobile represents.

To sum up: Nonfunctional, hence pathogenic consumption, is similar to having. Both types of experience weaken—or even destroy—man's productive development, deprive him of aliveness, and transform him into a thing. I hope the experience of having and nonfunctional consumption will still become clearer as we go on contrasting it with its opposite, the experience of being.

PART VI

17. From Having to Well-Being

If "well-being" (in the sense defined in the beginning of this book)—functioning well as a person, not as an instrument—is the supreme goal of one's efforts, two specific ways stand out that lead to the attainment of this goal: *Breaking through one's narcissism and breaking through the property structure of one's existence.*

Narcissism is an orientation in which all one's interest and passion are directed to one's own person: one's body, mind, feelings, interests, and so forth. Indeed, like Narcissus, the narcissistic person could be said to be in love with himself, if infatuation may be called love. For the narcissistic person, only he and what concerns him are fully real; what is outside, what concerns others, is real only in a superficial sense of perception; that is to say, it is real for one's senses and for one's intellect. But it is not real in a deeper sense, for our feeling or understanding. He is, in fact, aware only of what is outside, inasmuch as it affects him. Hence, he has no love, no compassion, no rational, objective judgment. The narcissistic person has built an invisible wall around himself. He is everything, the world is nothing. Or rather: He is the world.

The extreme examples of almost total narcissism are the newborn infant and the insane person; they both are incapable of relating to the world. (Actually, the insane person is not totally unrelated, as it was assumed by Freud and others; he has withdrawn. The infant cannot withdraw because it has not yet opened up anything beyond a solipsistic orientation. Freud referred to this difference by distinguishing between "primary" and "secondary" narcissism.) However, the fact has been neglected that the normal adult can also be narcissistic, even though not to the degree to be found in these extremes. Often he shows his narcissism quite openly, although he is not aware of being narcissistic. He thinks, speaks, and acts only in reference to himself, showing no really genuine interest in the world outside. On the contrary, the "great" man finds himself so interesting that it is only logical that he wants us to enjoy the manifestations of his greatness. If he is intelligent, witty, charming, powerful, rich, or famous, the average person will take no exception to his narcissistic exhibitionism. Many people, however, often try to hide their narcissism by being particularly modest and humble, or, in the subtle form being concerned with religious, occult, or political matters that all seem to point beyond the private interest.

Narcissism can hide in so many disguises that it can be said to be the most difficult of all psychic qualities to discover, and then only as a result of hard work and vigilance. Yet if one does not discover and reduce it considerably, the further way to self-completion is blocked.

Similar yet quite different from narcissism are egotism and selfishness, the results of the property, or having, mode of existence. A person living in this mode is not necessarily very narcissistic. He may have broken through the shell of his narcissism, have an adequate appreciation of reality outside himself, not necessarily be "in love with himself"; he knows who he is and who the others are, and can well distinguish between subjective experience and reality. Nevertheless, he wants everything for himself; has no pleasure in giving, in sharing, in solidarity, in cooperation, in love. He is a closed fortress, suspicious of others, eager to take and most reluctant to give. He represents, by and large, the anal-hoarding character. He is lonely, unrelated, and his strength lies in what he has and in the security of keeping it. On the other hand, the very narcissistic person is by no means necessarily selfish, egocentric, or property-oriented. He can be generous, giving, and tender, although all these characteristics must be qualified by the fact that to him the other person is not fully experienced as real. Yet one can easily observe very narcissistic persons whose spontaneous impulses are generous and giving rather than hoarding and holding. Since the two orientations—narcissism and selfishness—are rarely wholly differentiated, we must accept that, for growth, a double breakthrough is necessary: That through one's narcissism and that through one's having orientation.

The first condition for overcoming one's selfishness lies in the capacity of being aware of it. This is an easier task than the awareness of one's narcissism, because one's judgment is much less distorted, one can recognize facts more easily, and because it is less easy to hide. Of course, recognition of one's egocentricity is a *necessary* condition of overcoming it, but by no means a *sufficient* one. The second step to take is gaining an awareness of the roots of the having orientation, such as one's sense of powerlessness, one's fear of life, one's fear of the uncertain, one's distrust of people, and the many other subtle roots that have grown together so thickly that it often is impossible to uproot them.

Awareness of these roots is not sufficient condition, either. It must be accompanied by changes in *practice,* first of all by loosening the grip that selfishness has over one by beginning to let go. One must give up something, share, and go through the anxiety that these first little steps engender. One will discover, then, the fear of losing oneself that develops if one contemplates losing things, which function as props for one's sense of self. This implies not only giving up some possessions, but, even more important, habits, accustomed thoughts, identification with one's status, even phrases one is accustomed to hold on to, as well as the image that others may have of oneself (or that one hopes they have and tries to produce); in brief, if one tries to change routinized behavior in all spheres of life from breakfast routine to sex routine. In the process of trying to do so, anxieties are mobilized, and by not yielding to them confidence grows that the seemingly impossible can be done—and adventurousness grows. This process must be accompanied by attempting to go out of oneself and to turn to others. What does this mean? Something very simple, if we put it into words. One way of describing it is that our attention is drawn to others, to the world of nature, of

ideas, of art, of social and political events. We become "interested" in the world outside of our ego in the literal meaning of
interest, which comes from the Latin *inter esse,* i.e., "to be
among" or "to be over there," rather than to be shut in within
oneself. This development of "interest" can be compared to a
situation in which a person has seen and can describe a swimming
pool. He has spoken about it from the outside; his description
has been correct, yet without "interest." But when he has jumped
into the pool, and when he has become wet and *then* speaks
about the pool, he speaks as a different person about a different
pool. Now he and the pool are not opposing each other (although they have not become identical, either). The development
of interest means to jump and not to remain an outsider, an
observer, a person separated from what he sees. If a person has
the will and the determination to loosen the bars of his prison
of narcissism and selfishness, when he has the courage to tolerate
the intermittent anxiety, he experiences the first glimpses of joy
and strength that he sometimes attains. And only then a decisive
new factor enters into the dynamics of the process. This new
experience becomes the decisive motivation for going ahead and
following the path he has charted. Until then, his own dissatisfac-
tion and rational considerations of all kinds can guide him. But
these considerations can carry him only for a short while. They
will lose their power if the new element does not enter—experience of well-being—fleeting and small as it may be—which feels
so superior to anything experienced so far, that it becomes the
most powerful motivation for further progress—one that becomes stronger in and of itself the further progress goes on.

   To sum up once more: Awareness, will, practice, tolerance of
fear and of new experience, they are all necessary if transforma-
tion of the individual is to succeed. At a certain point the energy
and direction of inner forces have changed to the point where
an individual's sense of identity has changed, too. In the property
mode of existence the motto is: "I *am* what I *have*." After the
breakthrough it is "I am what I do" (in the sense of unalienated
activity); or simply, "I am what I am."

Bibliography

Bern, S. I. "Property," in P. Edwards (ed.), *The Encyclopedia of Philosophy*. New York: Macmillan Comp. and the Free Press, 1967.

Brooks, C. V. W. *Sensory Awareness: The Rediscovery of Experiencing*. New York: Viking, 1974.

Eckhart, Meister. *Meister Eckhart*, tr. C. de B. Evans, ed. Franz Pfeiffer. London: John M. Watkins, 1950.

Eckhart, Meister. *Meister Eckhart: A Modern Translation*, tr. R. B. Blakney. New York: Harper Torchbooks, Harper and Row, 1941.

Edwards, Paul, ed. *The Encyclopedia of Philosophy*. New York: Macmillan and The Free Press, 1967.

Fišer, Z. *Buddha*. Prague: Orbis, 1968.

Freud, S. *Character and Analeroticism*, S. E. Vol. 9, 1908.

Freud, S. *The Standard Edition of the Complete Psychological Works of Sigmund Freud* (S.E.), 24 Vols., ed. J. Strachey. London: Hogarth Press, 1953–74.

————. *The Origins of Psycho-Analysis*, S.E. Vol. 1 (1954).

————. *Character and Analeroticism*, S.E. Vol. 9 (1908).

Fromm, E. *The Anatomy of Human Destructiveness*. New York: Holt, Rinehart and Winston, 1973.

————. *Escape from Freedom*. New York: Farrar and Rinehart, 1941.

————. *The Forgotten Language: An Introduction to the Understanding of Dreams, Fairy Tales and Myths*. New York: Rinehart and Comp., 1951.

————. *Greatness and Limitations of Freud's Thought*. New York: Harper and Row, 1980.

————. *Man for Himself: An Inquiry into the Psychology of Ethics*. New York: Rinehart and Comp., 1947.

————. *The Sane Society*. New York: Rinehart and Winston, 1955.

————. *Sigmund Freud's Mission: An Analysis of His Personality and In-*

fluence. Vol. 21, ed. R. N. Anshen. New York: World Perspectives, Harper and Row, 1959.

————. *To Have or to Be?,* Vol. 50, ed. R. N. Anshen. New York: World Perspectives, Harper and Row, 1976.

Hegel, G. F. W. *Philosophy of Right,* Secs. 41, 45.

Horney, K. *Self-Analysis.* New York: W. W. Norton and Comp., 1942.

Illich, I. *Deschooling Society.* New York: Harper and Row, 1970.

————. *Medical Nemesis: The Expropriation of Health.* New York: Pantheon, 1976.

Kierkegaard, S. *Purity of Heart and to Will One Thing: Spiritual Preparation for the Office of Confession.* New York: Harper and Brothers, 1938.

Lazetto, M. C. *The Path of the Just Man,* 2nd ed., tr. S. Silverstein. Jerusalem and New York: Feldheim, 1974.

McGuire, W., ed. *The Freud/Jung Letters.* Princeton: Princeton University Press, 1974.

Marx, K. "Philosophical-Economical Manuscripts 1844," in E. Fromm, *Marx's Concept of Man.* New York: Frederick Ungar, 1961.

Mumford, L. *The Myth of the Machine: Techniques and Human Development.* New York: Harcourt, Brace and World, 1967.

Nyanaponika, M. *The Heart of Buddhist Meditation.* New York: Samuel Weiser, 1973.

Spinoza, B. de. *Ethics.* New York: Oxford University Press, 1927.

Grundlagen des Fortschritts bestätigt durch wissenschaftliche Untersuchungen in die Transzendentale Meditation. Los Angeles: Maharishi International University, 1974.

Turnbull, C. M. *Wayward Servants: The Two Worlds of the African Pygmies.* London: Eyre and Spottiswoode, 1965.

Index